Lori Reid has written a number of books and numerous magazine articles on Chinese and Western Astrology, Personal Development, and Hand Analysis. She is a professional hand analyst who is consulted by people form all over the world, and who makes regular radio and television appearances. The author of *Chinese Horoscopes for Lovers* and *The Complete Book Chinese Horoscopes*.

The *Elements of* is a series designed to present high quality introductions to a broad range of essential subjects.

The books are commissioned specifically from experts in their fields. They provide readable and often unique views of the various topics covered, and are therefore of interest both to those who have some knowledge of the subject, as well as to those who are approaching it for the first time.

Many of these concise yet comprehensive books have practical suggestions and exercises which allow personal experience as well as theoretical understanding, and offer a valuable source of information on many important themes.

In the same series

> **the elements of**

handreading

lori reid

ELEMENT

Shaftesbury, Dorset • Rockport, Massachusetts • Brisbane, Queensland

© Element Books Limited, 1994
Text © Lori Reid 1994

First published in Great Britain in 1994 by
Element Books Limited
Shaftesbury, Dorset SP7 8BP

Published in the USA in 1994 by
Element Books, Inc.
PO Box 830, Rockport, MA 01966

Published in Australia in 1992 by
Element Books and distributed
by Penguin Books Australia Ltd
487 Maroondah Highway, Ringwood,
Victoria 3134

Reprinted 1996
Reissued 1997

Cover design by Max Fairbrother
Typeset by The Electronic Book Factory Ltd, Fife, Scotland
Printed and bound in Great Britain by
Biddles Ltd, Guildford and King's Lynn

British Library Cataloguing in Publication
data available

Library of Congress Cataloging in Publication
data available

ISBN 1–86204–075–3

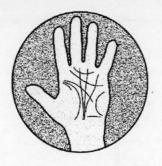

CONTENTS

LIST OF FIGURES

LIST OF PRINTS

To my dear sister Gianna
with love

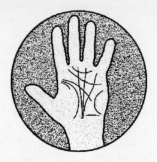

1 · INTRODUCTION

Do you enjoy a good detective story? A thriller where you have to work out 'whodunnit' by the subtle clues that are carefully dotted about? If you do, you'll enjoy reading hands.

Handreading, or hand analysis as it is also known these days, is the modern scientific approach to the old study of palmistry. We don't know exactly how the practice began, or where it first occurred. But we do know that cave men were interested enough in their hands to paint them on the walls of their caves, and some of the earliest evidence may be found in the Altamira caves near Santander in northern Spain.

We shall never know if our early cave-dwelling ancestors actually *read* their hands fifteen thousand years ago, or whether they were merely cataloguing their world onto their walls, but the first tangible evidence that markings in the hands were seriously studied, and the information used analytically, is found in ancient Hindu scriptures dating back to the second millenium BC. The fact that actual laws governing the reading of hands were written down must mean that the practice had already been in existence for some considerable while.

Certainly at that time its use was widespread throughout the East, and knowledge of the principles of handreading soon spread from Asia Minor to Ancient Greece. Plato, Aristotle, Hippocrates and Ptolemaeus all knew, studied, used and wrote about palmistry. Galen, the father of medicine, used the markings in the hand both for diagnostic purposes, as indicators of health, as well as for character analysis.

From Ancient Greece the knowledge was brought to the Roman Empire, and from there to the rest of Europe. Julius Caesar was well acquainted with handreading, as were Virgil, Pliny and the Emperor Augustus.

Up to this time handreading had been highly regarded, was taught at the great learning institutions of the ancient world and was used extensively by physicians, philosophers and learned men. It is still held in the same high regard in the Orient where, it is believed, its origins lie. But in the Dark Ages of northern Europe, however, the practice of reading hands fell foul of the Christian Church and was subsequently driven underground. From then to this day it has enjoyed, in the West, a somewhat chequered career: alternately condemned and derided, outlawed and esteemed.

In the Middle Ages the Church banned handreading altogether, and excommunicated its practitioners. During Henry VIII's reign, laws were passed that prohibited its use; if found, those who read hands were branded as sorcerers, and could expect due retribution. It is to its lasting credit, and perhaps a tribute to its validity, that despite all attempts by either the Church or Parliament to suppress its use, handreading is not only still with us but is actually flourishing today.

It is significant that one of the first books published, in the mid 1400s, was on handreading. In the seventeenth century, palmistry was one of the subjects to be found in the curricula of many German universities. With the Victorian preoccupation for scientific discovery, handreading flourished and scores of new books and treatises on the subject swelled the bookshop shelves. One of the most famous practitioners of that time was Count Louis Hamon, or Cheiro, as he is more popularly known.

At the turn of the century another branch of handreading, fingerprinting, was validated and adopted by Scotland Yard for forensic purposes. Dermatoglyphics, the medical name for fingerprints and general skin ridge patterns, was extensively investigated throughout the first half of the twentieth century by medical researchers who discovered a correlation between genetic factors and the skin patterns in our hands.

Today, with modern psychological techniques, handreading has developed into a valuable analytical tool, and is enjoying a new upsurge of interest not only in the fields of medicine and psychoanalysis but also amongst the general public. Perhaps, as we near the twenty-first century, the new approach that analysts are taking to reading hands will help to restore its credibility, and re-establish the status it once enjoyed in past millenia.

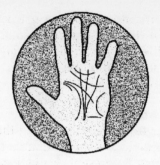

2 · HAND ANALYSIS

Hand analysis is a complex investigative process, a piece of detective work, by which information about an individual is slowly collated through the meticulous study of his or her hands.

A good analysis of a hand can provide a wealth of information about its owner. It can reveal character traits, attitudes, behaviour, motivation, and the way an individual thinks. It can give valuable insights into how that person relates to others, and the expectations that person will have of those relationships – both romantic and otherwise!

A good analysis can explain a person's potential, reveal innate gifts and talents, and can expose inherited qualities that are lying dormant, ready to be developed. The general state of mind and body will show up clearly, often giving the subject time to take the necessary action to improve the situation. Finally, the hand can yield important clues about the possible opportunities, events or results of actions and decisions which are likely to be taken in the future.

There are serious applications, too, for handreading in both the psychological and medical fields. Psychologically, this type of analysis could be an invaluable aid in the understanding of personality and motivation, and could certainly be used to help sort out problems and behavioural difficulties. In medicine, the practice could be used as a diagnostic tool. Indeed, much medical research involving fingerprints and genetic diseases has already been carried out, and current studies are showing correlations between abnormal skin patterns and heart disease. Certainly, hand analysis could play an increasingly useful role in this field.

BODY CHEMISTRY

Why the character of an individual, and the likely events of his or her life, should be stamped into the hand, is still open to speculation. At present, we believe that there must be a connection between our body chemistry and the natural electrical impulses that we emit which imprint their messages, not only onto the hand, but elsewhere on our bodies too.

It's well known that the palm contains a vast concentration of nerve endings – more, apart from the sole of the foot, than any other part of the body – which makes it a superb receptor upon which our electrical impulses can be registered. Because the hand has been closely studied for thousands of years, all the while correlating events to markings, a valuable and accurate record of the interpretation of those markings has been built up.

The idea that our body chemistry should be responsible for printing such information on our hands is not quite so far-fetched as it sounds when we consider some of the other oddities that go on in our bodies, often without our knowledge. Consider, for instance, some of the symptoms which are recognized pointers to disease: yellowing eyeballs as a sign of jaundice; hair loss and bulging eyes in cases of hyperthyroidism; and an array of odd allergic reactions which, even now, can't be fully explained. Why on earth, we might ask, should a complaint of the liver produce yellow eyeballs, or why should eating seafood bring some people out in a rash as if they had just run through a field of stinging nettles?

Unless we understand our body mechanisms, these apparently unconnected symptoms must seem very odd indeed. In just the same way it seems strange that patterns of our lives should somehow be transmitted to and inscribed in our hands; yet thousands of years' worth of observation tells us it is so.

THE ANALYTICAL PROCEDURE

The study of the hand is conducted on several levels. No one factor stands alone; each part modifies, confirms and corroborates every other until a profile of the individual is built up.

FIRST LEVEL

The first level is the analysis of the shape of the hand. This lays down the basic character, and together with the actual structure and formation of the palm and fingers, the nails, the colour, the texture and even the temperature must be assessed at this stage.

SECOND LEVEL

The second level is the analysis of the skin markings, and this information is superimposed onto the first level. When considering the skin markings, not only are the well-known and easily recognizable fingerprints examined, but the entire skin patterning that covers the whole of the palm is looked at in minute detail too. The modern term for the fingerprints and all the patterns created by the actual skin ridges is dermatoglyphics.

THIRD LEVEL

The third level deals with the way the hands are held, and the stance that the fingers take. It is now widely accepted that gesture is an important clue to personality and make-up and, even if the hand is only being examined from a print, the way it has been placed on paper, the stance of the fingers and the relation of the thumb to the palm must all be taken into consideration.

FOURTH LEVEL

Finally, the lines are examined in terms of their course and structure. Incidental markings, either standing independently on the hand or lying across the lines, are also investigated in minute detail.

By taking each step one at a time, and superimposing the information gleaned at each operation, a clear 'photofit' picture of the individual's character and personality will slowly emerge.

OUR CHANGING LINES

Contrary to popular opinion, lines in our hands can and do change. This can sometimes happen quite quickly: for example, stress markings across the finger tips. These changes in the lines occur according to our experiences, influences, and relationships which colour our understanding and perspective. Our conscious decisions, positive thinking, changes of environment and life-styles, states of mind and health all contribute their own subtle patterns in our hands. This all goes to prove that as living, thinking, feeling human beings we have the power not only to choose but also to make our own destinies.

Essentially, the hand is a useful guide to the understanding of our character and personality, and it acts as an indicator of the possibilities and future events that are likely to touch our lives. But the fundamental principle that must always be borne is mind is that we have free will, and we can decide for ourselves whether to develop the potential that is shown, to accept blindly any of the future prospects or to actively intervene.

For example, should a future negative event marking be detected in a hand, it is possible that its owner may be able to steer clear of the circumstances that would cause that problem. Perhaps he or she might be able to skirt around the event or, if not, at least being warned about it gives the individual advance notice to work out a coping strategy. Forewarned is forearmed.

On the positive side, of course, markings in the hand can alert us to future opportunities. With this knowledge an individual might strive towards them and be aware of when they are likely to turn up, and so not let them inadvertently slip through the net.

LEFT- AND RIGHT-HANDEDNESS

Misconceptions about the meaning of right- and left-handedness abound. Psychological studies in this area have shown that the hands correspond to the right and left hemispheres of the brain. Interestingly, each hemisphere carries out discrete

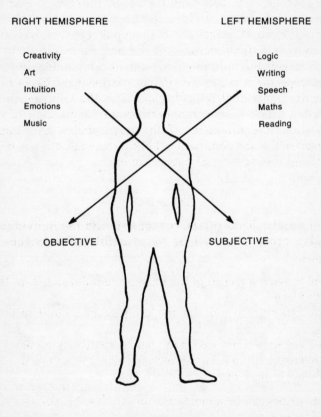

Figure 1. Left- and Right-handedness

and unique functions. On a right-hander, the left deals with the more hard-core functions of logic, writing, speech, maths and reading, generally speaking, all the rational or 'masculine' processes of the brain. The right hemisphere deals with such functions as our intuitive or emotional responses and our ability to be creative and to appreciate art and music. In short, the softer or more 'feminine' processes.

As Figure 1 shows, the messages from each half of the brain are crossed over so that the right hemisphere dominates the left side of the body, and the left hemisphere governs the right side. Therefore the right hand represents the functions of the left-brain hemisphere, and the left hand represents the functions of the right hemisphere. So, when it comes to analyzing the hands of a right-hander, it is the right or dominant hand which reveals the individual's objective, conscious self: what is known as the *persona*. The left, or passive, hand reveals the subjective, emotional, subconscious side: the *anima*.

For left-handers, who number around 13 per cent of the population, the functions of the hemispheres are simply reversed so that the dominant or left side becomes the objective hand, and the right is the subjective one.

TAKING A PRINT

Taking regular hand prints, perhaps around the individual's birthday every year, can be very useful for a number of reasons:

- they provide a record of the changes and development that take place
- they can help to monitor the progress of a child through life
- they are sometimes easier to analyze than a living hand
- they enable more accurate measurements to be taken
- they are a mark of a person's identity

Taking prints can be a messy business since it involves using printing inks or even lipstick, which can make a very acceptable substitute. The best ink is water-soluble lino printing ink, which can be washed off the hands with soap and water. If

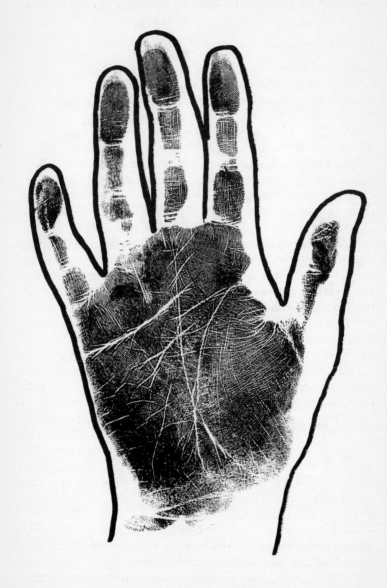

Print 1. A Clear Print

using the lipstick method, the darker the lipstick, the better the results. Print 1 shows the sort of clarity you should aim for.

Materials required

Lino printing ink – water-soluble (or lipstick)
Printer's roller (or rolling pin/empty bottle)
Sheet of glass (or sheet of silver foil/glossy magazine)
A4 paper
Table knife
Sharp pencil
Folded towel
Tissues/cotton-wool

Procedure

1. Squeeze a small amount of ink onto the glass, and roll out thinly with the roller, wrapped in clingfilm.
2. Roll the inked roller evenly all over the fingers and palm, and down to cover about the first inch (2–3 cm) of the wrist. If using lipstick, apply thinly and evenly with tissues or cotton-wool.
3. Place the sheet of paper over the folded towel, and place the hand in as natural a position as possible on the paper. If, on lifting up the hand, the central part of the palm has not printed, remove the towel and place the paper directly on the table. Re-ink the hand and place it on the paper. Now, slip the table knife underneath and press up into the hollow of the palm. If that doesn't work, a last resort that should get results is to work the other way up. When the hand has been re-inked, place it on the table, palm-side up, and lay the paper carefully on top, pressing it firmly over the hand. You must ensure that you don't move the paper as you press it down onto the palm, or the print will smudge.
4. Next, lightly ink the thumb tip and press it onto a corner of each sheet: the right thumb on the right-handed prints, and the left thumb on the left-handed prints.
5. Several clear prints of each hand should be taken. Each palm print should be carefully marked with the **date**, the

owner's **name, date of birth, gender** and whether **right-** or **left-handed**.

6. When the hands are washed and dried and the inked print is also dry, re-position the hand over each print and draw around the outline with a sharp pencil or ballpoint. The advantage of taking the print on the hard table top without a towel underneath is that the outline can be pencilled in at the same time as the print is being taken.

PHOTOCOPIES

If it's not possible to take a hand print, a good photocopy can be used as a substitute. Unlike inked prints, though, the very fine detail of the palmar lines and skin patterns are unlikely to show up clearly using this method. However, in an emergency or as a back-up to prints, photocopies are very useful.

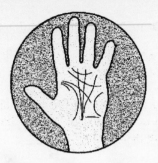

3 · HANDS IN THEIR ELEMENTS

The shape of a hand determines the basic character of the individual. It is the shape that establishes the fundamental bottom line, the foundation characteristics, if you like, upon which the personal profile of an individual is built up.

Although every hand is individual – a person's right hand will not exactly match the left – it is possible to classify all hands, according to their general shape, into four distinct groups. These are known as the **Earth, Air, Fire** and **Water** categories (see Figure 2). Each group is defined by the shape of the palm in relation to the length of the fingers. The answers to two questions will determine the category: is the palm square or oblong; are the fingers long or short? Digits are considered long if the middle finger is as long as, or longer than, three-quarters the length of the palm. When less than three-quarters, the fingers are short.

These four permutations of square or oblong palms together with long or short fingers produce the following four categories:

- •square palm + short fingers = Earth hand
- •square palm + long fingers = Air hand
- •oblong palm + short fingers = Fire hand
- •oblong palm + long fingers = Water hand

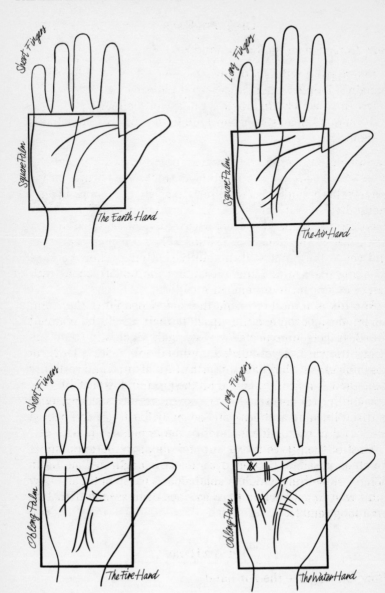

Figure 2. The Earth, Air, Fire and Water Hands

THE EARTH HAND

How to recognize the Earth hand

- square palm with short fingers
- mainly loop or whorl finger-print patterns
- few lines which are all strong and well-defined
- the hand is clear, strong and solid with a look of competence about it

Earth-handed people are practical, down-to-earth, pragmatic types. Stable, reliable and solid as rock, they work prodigiously hard and, because they tend to be plodding and methodical, what they lack in imagination, they certainly make up for in practical expertise. They approach life in a level-headed, no-nonsense fashion. They are plain speakers and get to the point with no shilly-shallying. Their habit of speaking their minds and presenting the unvarnished truth can often appear blunt and insensitive.

Routine is important to Earth-handed people to the point where they become quite upset if their carefully planned schedule gets unexpectedly disturbed. Generally, they are straightforward, level-headed, rational folk with plenty of common sense. They have an earthy turn of mind and certainly have their feet firmly planted on the ground. Respectable and law-abiding themselves, they lay great store in a strong sense of discipline and authority and so many Earth-handed people are found in the police force or in the armed services.

Most of them love to get out and about in the open air as much as possible. If cooped up for any length of time in an office – something which is anathema to many of them – they can't wait to get back to their gardens or to stretch their legs on a long ramble.

THE AIR HAND

How to recognize the Air hand

- square palm with long fingers
- mainly loop finger-print patterns
- several, clear and well-formed lines

- the hand feels wiry and appears 'clean' and confident

Air-handed people are life's communicators. They possess lively, intelligent minds with an insatiable curiosity that makes them take an interest in everything that is going on around them. Because of their bird-like attention and restless mentality, they thrive in a buzzy atmosphere that hums with activity. Meeting challenges and having the sort of job that requires staying one step ahead of the game is perfect for these people. Variety and change are meat and drink to them, whilst routine and the monotony of the 9-to-5 existence completely stultifies their imagination.

With their mercurial minds they are quick learners and make excellent students. Computers, hi-tech equipment and all sorts of modern gadgetry fascinate them. But they are perhaps at their best working with other people, and are particularly skilled at dealing with the general public. That's why so many of them are found in the media, in the publishing business, or in the travel industry where they can also put their linguistic skills into practice.

On the whole, they are emotionally well-balanced, and because they are able to keep their feelings under control they can come across as cool and distant.

THE FIRE HAND

How to recognize the Fire hand

- oblong palm with short fingers
- several whorl finger-print patterns
- many lines which are strong and well-defined
- the palm appears busy but structured, whilst the hand has a lively and energetic feel to it

Bright, intelligent, energetic, dynamic and vital characterizes those with the Fire hand. Full of drive and enthusiasm, these fun-loving people are able to infect others with their excitement and supreme optimism. Best in the full glare of the spotlight, they shine when they are given the approval and adulation of the crowd. That's why so many of them find a natural place for their talents in 'show biz' and in the entertainment world in general.

Because of their boundless energy, people with fire-shaped hands make excellent sportsmen and women. Because they are pioneers at heart, they are never happier than when at the forefront of the action: they will be the record-breakers, they will set the standards, or strive to be at the very cutting edge of their professions.

In all areas, they make excellent leaders, able to inspire and motivate those under them. They are strong and positive individuals, excitable and volatile with a tendency to live life in the fast lane. But the danger from this penchant for high living is that unless they learn how to pace themselves sensibly many of them will simply burn themselves out.

THE WATER HAND

How to recognize the Water hand

- long palm with long fingers
- mainly loop finger-print patterns
- a profusion of fine, spidery lines
- an elegant hand with an air of fragility about it

Because of its lack of substance and robustness, the Water hand tells of a sensitive, emotional and highly-strung nature. People who possess this hand shape are thoughtful and contemplative and, as such, become the poets, the dreamers, the visionaries amongst us. Indeed, this is the least materialistic of all the shapes and water-handed people are gentle, passive, spiritual individuals who tend to live life with their heads in the clouds.

Creative and highly artistic, many are attracted to the music industry and to the Arts. In general, these are cultured and urbane people with refined tastes and a strong sense for the aesthetics. They can lose themselves for hours in fine detail and minutiae. But, if not involved in the arts, many will be found in the caring professions where their compassionate natures will find a ready outlet.

Water-handed folk are the least able to cope with stress

17

and pressure. At work and at home they require a peaceful environment, since tranquillity and harmony are essential to their well-being. Because of their other-worldliness and their unrealistic and impractical dispositions, many in this category are unsuited to the materialistic demands of everyday life. Moreover, with their impressionability and their tendency to be influenced, they must take care not to allow themselves to be easily led by stronger, more forceful personalities.

THE MOUNTS

The mounts, Figure 3, are the fleshy pads that sit on the surface of the palm, to cover and cushion the nerve endings and blood vessels in the hand. There are several of them, each one representing certain qualities according to its position on the palm. The way we express or bring to life those qualities is revealed by the way the mount is formed and presented.

The mounts should, generally speaking, be springy – not too hard, nor too soft – and this applies especially so to the basal ones of Venus and Luna. Too soft and the person is indolent, self-centred, a sensualist, a dreamer. Too hard and we have someone who is a tough realist; someone who is pragmatic and phlegmatic in the extreme.

A good 'rule of thumb' to remember is that a high, well-shaped mount denotes quality: that is, integrity and discriminative tastes. A shapeless but large expanse, however, means quantity, often at the expense of quality.

Assessing which of the mounts in a hand are more, or less, developed in comparison to each other is important because this will point out not only *which* aspects of life are of greater (or lesser) significance in that individual's life, but also *how* the qualities represented by a particular mount are expressed.

THE MOUNT OF VENUS

The Mount of Venus comprises the ball of the thumb, that fleshy area inside the Life line. According to its development, it reveals the individual's sense of being and gusto for living.

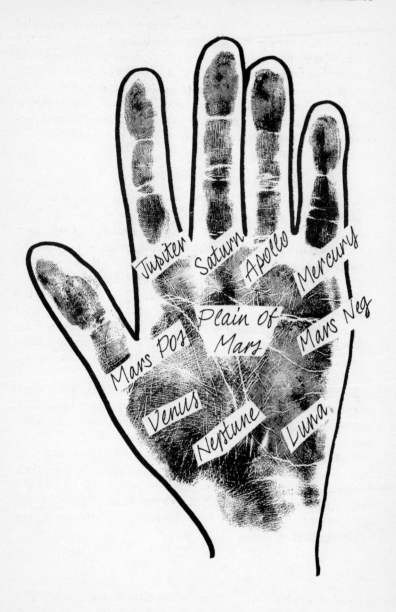

Figure 3. The Mounts

Full and round
vibrant, enthusiastic, outgoing
full of life, virile, vital
plenty of energy
ability to bounce back physically and emotionally
warm-hearted
loving, attractive personality
sunny disposition
need to be loved

Narrow and flat
lack of vitality
low energy levels
vulnerability to ill-health and general malaise
poor resistance to disease
poor recuperative powers
cool and reserved

Springy to the touch
lively, energetic, dynamic
brimming with health
on the ball

Soft and flabby
self-centred
preference for a soft, easy life
lazy
sensual

Excessively large
exaggerated actions, emotions and appetites
apparently 'larger than life'
boastful
uncontrollable desires

If in doubt as to the fullness of this mount, simply check the course of the Life line skirting around it. For indications of good, healthy mental and physical well-being, the line should swing out clearly to the centre of the palm. If, however, the line skirts closely around the base of the thumb it reveals someone who is reserved, not very robust at all and with a strong tendency to a cynical disposition.

THE MOUNT OF LUNA

On the opposite side to Venus is found the Mount of Luna. This is the area at the base of the percussion which lies just above the wrist. It represents imagination, intuition and generally, the subconscious.

Well-developed
sensitive
receptive to moods, impressions, vibrations and atmosphere
feeling for Nature
warm and sympathetic
natural ability to empathize with others
imaginative

Low-set into the wrist
in tune with natural rhythms
psychic
sense of balance and poise (models/dancers have this formation)
supersensitive to vibrations

Forming a high dome
heightened perception
marked imagination

Large and soft
dreamer
indolent
prone to moods
tendency to melancholia or depression

Insignificant
lack of imagination
conservative

conformist mentality
emotionally cool and distant

THE MOUNT OF NEPTUNE

Between the Mounts of Venus and Luna is situated the Mount of Neptune. A fully-developed mount here is a rare find.

Well-developed
magnetic personality
charismatic
spiritual
interests in mysticism
powers of ESP

Wide but flat
lack of self-reflection

UPPER MARS

The area of Upper Mars is found directly above the Luna mount, and it represents moral courage, and the subject's degree of tolerance, persistence and resistance.

Well-developed
powers of endurance in the face of difficulties
strong moral principles
high pain threshold

Weak and flat
lack of moral fibre
lack of integrity
moral cowardice
low tolerance to pain

LOWER MARS

The Mount of Lower Mars is found above Venus, inside the top part of the Life line. Whereas Upper Mars represents moral fortitude, this mount tells of physical courage and prowess.

Excessively developed
courage
fighting spirit
argumentativeness
aggression
love of challenge
dare-devilry

Under-developed
lack of courage

Well-proportioned
sporty
active, energetic
physically able to handle oneself
good balance between courage and prudence

THE PLAIN OF MARS

This is the area which bridges the gap between Upper and Lower Mars. It has become known as the reservoir of energy, and you can gauge its depth and thickness by holding it between your finger and thumb.

Soft and spongy
lazy
self-indulgent
selfish

Thin
a lack of common sense
egocentric

Thick and well-padded
resourceful
astute

THE MOUNT OF JUPITER

This mount lies directly below the index finger and it repesents the ego, one's standing and sense of ambition in the world.

Well-proportioned
fine sense of justice
high moral standards
self-respect
self-esteem
good sense of identity
reasoned understanding of one's strengths and weaknesses

Over-developed
arrogant
self-important
self-opinionated
pompous

Flat
a worrier
easily influenced

THE MOUNT OF SATURN

This mount, beneath the middle finger, represents several diverse aspects of life: stability, property, the basic requirements for living, agriculture, sometimes study and philosophy, occasionally music too. It is psychologically healthier if this mount is not well-developed.

Large or high
gloomy
melancholic
pessimistic
'misery-guts'
unsociable
misanthropist

Gently rounded
love of research
scholar
accomplished musician
interest in the paranormal and occult

THE MOUNT OF APOLLO

Lying at the root of the ring finger, the Mount of Apollo is associated with creativity and the arts, happiness, satisfaction and success.

Well-proportioned
warm
generous
sunny disposition
popular
attractive personality
lucky

Over large
garish tastes
'flash Harry' type
extravagant
desirous of attention
a prey to flattery

Under-developed
frugal
lack of aesthetic appreciation

THE MOUNT OF MERCURY

This mount under the little finger, represents communication and personal expression.

Well-proportioned
love of freedom
easy communicator
able to put others at their ease
warm and friendly
business sense

Over large
nervous energy
need of stimulation
low boredom-threshold

Under-developed
lacks self-confidence
easily tongue-tied
fear of ridicule
shy and self-conscious.

Too high
garrulous
over-fond of gossiping

DIVISION OF THE PALM

When looking at a hand it is possible to see at a glance which aspects of life are salient to that individual. This is done by dividing the palm, first vertically and then horizontally, in order to establish where the greater development, and hence the greater emphasis, lies.

THE VERTICAL DIVISIONS

This reveals differences in emphasis between the rational and instinctive sides of the personality. The dividing line (see Figure 4), is drawn from the wrist up to the web between the middle and ring fingers. The part of the palm that lies on the radial, or thumb side, of the line represents the ego, the conscious or rational self. The other half, towards the percussion, is known as the ulna side and represents the subconscious or instinctive part of the personality.

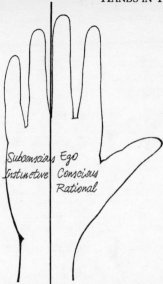

Figure 4. The Vertical Divisions

If the half of the hand that's on the thumb side appears better developed than the other, the dominant preoccupations of that individual revolve around the more concrete, mundane and materialistic concerns of everyday life. Conscious, logical, rational and tangible affairs in life will predominate.

If, however, the ulna side appears fuller and more generously endowed, it will be the subconscious, intuitive or imaginative side of the personality that takes precedence over all other aspects of life. The development here reveals that it is the soul, the spiritual or creative elements which matter most in that individual's life, and which are far more important than anything material or worldly.

THE HORIZONTAL DIVISIONS

The palm may be divided horizontally into three separate areas as shown in Figure 5.

The bottom third (comprising the Mounts of Luna, Neptune and Venus) represents vital energy, physical strength and robustness. Here can be seen the *capacity* for living. This

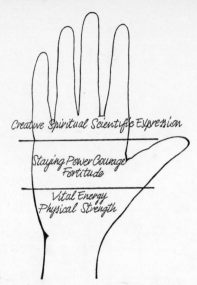

Figure 5. The Horizontal Divisions

band represents the body's energy stores. Well-developed, it highlights a strong, physical and energetic person, with a passionate zest for life, possibly sporty, certainly earthy. When there is a lack of development here, so that the palm tapers thinly down towards the wrist, it reveals someone who is lacking in stamina and not physically very robust, who needs plenty of rest in order to conserve his or her energies.

The central part of the palm (comprising the two Mounts and Plain of Mars) represents staying power, physical courage, aggression and dare-devilry, together with moral integrity and fortitude. If this area appears stronger than either of the other two, the individual is well-endowed with all these characteristics. Perhaps a true, brave, uncompromising leader of men, a Spartacus or a St Joan, might have had this sort of formation.

The band right across the top of the palm (comprising the mounts beneath the fingers) represents how we express ourselves creatively, spiritually and scientifically. If the whole palm broadens out towards the fingers so that the greatest width is at the top, it suggests that intellectual pursuits and interests predominate.

THE PERCUSSION EDGE

Careful analysis of the percussion edge will reveal a good deal about an individual's powers of creativity.

Jutting out beneath the little finger If the palm noticeably bulges outwards here (see Print 2), it's a sign of a person who is highly strung or who lives on his or her nerves. These are mental fidgets who are forever thinking and planning ahead, who find it hard to switch off. Such people tend to let their minds drive their bodies on, and must take care not to exhaust themselves physically or mentally. Sound advice to these people is to practise some tension-release or deep-breathing exercises, and maybe some simple yoga techniques in order to calm their over-active minds.

The whole percussion curves outwards If the whole edge of the palm forms a bow window effect it is the mark of creativity (see Print 3). People with this formation are also highly intuitive and may even experience colourful and prophetic dreams. They should learn to rely on their instincts and inner feelings as these will be an invaluable guide to them through life.

Developed at the base When the greatest development is seen lower down by the wrist, it highlights excellent physical resources and is the sort of formation typically seen on the hands of sportsmen and women: the active, energetic types who prefer the outdoor life.

Straight A straight, flat percussion edge reveals a lack of physical stamina and staying power. There may also be a want of imagination and the intuitive faculties may be under-developed.

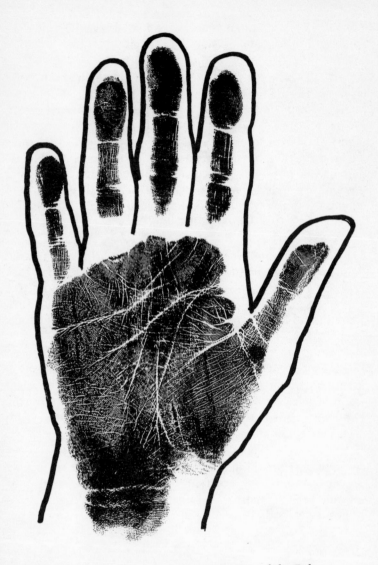

Print 2. Percussion Bulging at the Top of the Palm

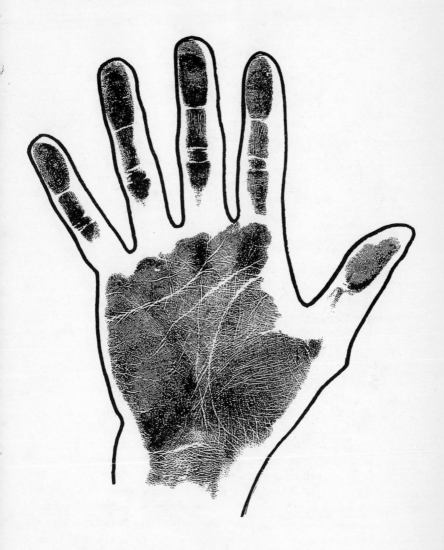

Print 3. Curved Percussion

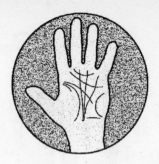

4 · ALL FINGERS AND THUMBS

Fingers may be referred to as the index, middle, ring and little fingers. Alternatively, many hand analysts call them by their classical names: Jupiter, Saturn, Apollo and Mercury. These are simply a form of shorthand which pinpoints the principles that are represented by each digit.

PHALANGES

Each finger is made up of three phalanges; the top, or nail, phalanx; the middle; and the bottom. The top phalanx represents the mental, spiritual and emotional expression of the particular finger; the middle tells how that expression is practically applied; and the bottom phalanx reveals the physical or material attitude.

If the middle phalanges are shorter than both the top and bottom ones it is a sign of the dreamer; someone who has good ideas, but who doesn't bring them to fruition. When the top phalanges are the longest, the individual will take a more intellectual than practical outlook in life. When the middle phalanges are the longest, it is in the managerial or practical abilities that the individual excels. Full, rounded or well-developed basal phalanges (see Print 4) usually signify

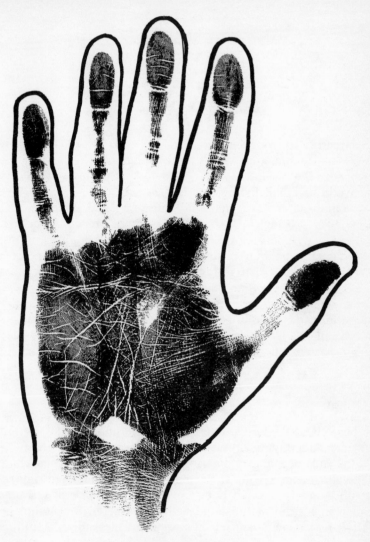

Print 4. *Full Basal Phalanges*

Figure 6. Droplet

an earthy or even a materialistic outlook. They also suggest a sensual, sometimes self-indulgent nature. The podgier the fingers, the easier and softer and more luxurious their owners would like their lives to be.

Opposite to these are the thin, firm fingers which represent a more sparing, more frugal and more spiritual outlook. People with thin fingers can exist quite happily without too many material chattels, and are able to tighten their belts philosophically when times are hard. Quality matters far more to them than quantity.

Sometimes little rounded pads that look like drops of water are formed on the finger tips (Figure 6). Appropriately these are called droplets, and they reveal an individual with a very sensitive touch. Such people have heightened tactile senses.

FINGER LENGTHS

The longer the fingers the more patient and painstaking the individual (Figure 7a). Long-fingered people focus their attention and are able to sit for ages pouring over fine, intricate and elaborate work. They have an eye for detail and need time to think and to ponder. Long fingers are the mark of the fine craftsman, the mathematician, logician or anyone found in occupations requiring concentration and meticulous attention to detail.

Short-fingered people (Figure 7b) take a broader view. Red-tape frustrates them and pedantic nit-picking rankles sorely. Short fingers point to impulsive, instinctive and intuitive types. These people go for the overall view rather than homing in on the finer points, and they are excellent at

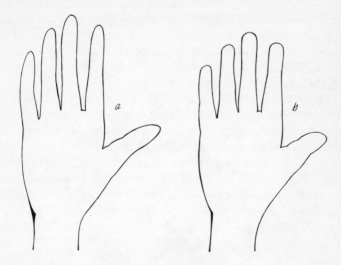

Figure 7. Finger Lengths

making plans and initiating projects, preferring to leave the minor details to their longer-fingered colleagues. Don't ever expect short-fingered people to go by the rule book – this is much too slow for them. Nor do they suffer fools gladly!

The next step is to take each finger in turn, to analyze its strengths and weaknesses and to see it in relation to its neighbours.

JUPITER OR THE INDEX FINGER

In classical mythology, Jupiter was the chief god and ruler of the world. As applied to hand reading, this finger is basically known as the 'me' finger. It represents:

- the ego
- the conscious self in the environment
- attitudes to one's position or standing in the world
- sense of leadership
- interests in politics
- interests in religion
- interests in the law

35

A straight, well-set index shows a healthy ego. It reveals a goodly amount of self-esteem and self-respect, together with a feeling of being in control of one's own destiny. If it leans outwards, towards the thumb, it denotes a strong ambitious streak. The goals, aims and objectives of the ambition are dependent on the rest of the hand.

An over-long index (see Print 5), that is, one which is either as long as or even longer than the middle finger, denotes a need for power and control over others. On a good hand, this is the sign of an excellent leader of men. But on a bad hand, one which shows weaknesses, misplaced aggression or vices, this formation can highlight the plain bully and the dictator.

A very short index, that is, considerably shorter than the ring finger, denotes a lack of self-confidence and a feeling of

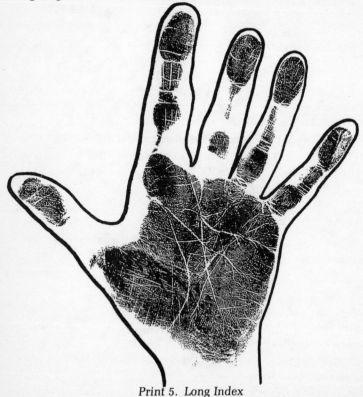

Print 5. Long Index

inadequacy. People with this feature are often self-conscious and seem unable to control their own destinies. Moreover, if it is deeply set into the palm there could be a strong inferiority complex, producing the 'chip on the shoulder' type.

When the tip bends noticeably towards Saturn it tells of a person who likes to work quietly behind the scenes rather than in the full glare of the limelight. There is a strong dislike of competition, and anything of a cut-throat, rat-race nature should be avoided at all costs.

Long top phalanges here emphasize interests or involvement in politics, religion and the law. Many vicars, military leaders, politicians, lawyers, judges, policemen and women display this particular feature on their indeces. Long middle phalanges are the mark of the executive. Long basal phalanges belong to trainers and managers in the sports world. Full or broad indeces identify those in the catering industries, chefs, restaurateurs or anyone who has a great appreciation of good food.

SATURN OR THE MIDDLE FINGER

Saturn was the mythological father of Jupiter and so has become associated with old age and contemplative study. For the purposes of hand analysis this finger is linked to:

- one's idea of security
- attitudes to stability, commitment and responsibility
- the basic essentials of life
- property
- agriculture, farming and the land
- mining
- conservation
- research
- history and tradition

A very long middle finger denotes a 'Saturnine' disposition, someone who is melancholy, down in the mouth, a bit of a wet blanket, possibly depressive and rather fixed in temperament. A short middle finger highlights the Bohemian type, one who flouts traditions, rules and customs. People with very short Saturn fingers especially loathe red-tape and petty bureaucracy.

A long top phalanx here shows a love of research. Interests in alternative beliefs and in the paranormal are also revealed. A long middle phalanx is the mark of the efficient manager or housekeeper. Mathematicians, accountants, historians, scientists or physicists may also possess this formation, as might farmers and conservationists. Long basal phalanges show a concern for physical and material security: land, property and money.

APOLLO OR THE RING FINGER

In legend, Apollo was the god who drove the sun across the heavens in his golden chariot, and was associated with music and poetry, prophecy and healing. In hand analysis this finger represents:

- creativity
- the Arts
- sense of happiness and fulfilment
- success

A long ring finger, one that is longer than the middle finger, is the sign of the gambler, the over-confident speculator. This doesn't just apply to punters – those who like a bet or two on the horses – it can just as easily apply to anyone who is prepared to take risks and chances in life. If very short, it reveals a lack of creative talent; possibly someone who doesn't have any true appreciation of the arts.

A long top phalanx shows an intellectual approach to art. A broad or spatulate tip is interesting as it is a sign of dramatic ability; actors and actresses invariably have a spatulate-tipped Apollo finger. There may also be a tendency to exaggeration. If the middle phalanx is long and lean it reveals an eye for detail, line, colour and perspective. A long basal phalanx shows good artistic taste. A plump and well-developed phalanx (see Print 6) highlights the 'collector's urge'. As such it may pinpoint the selective and discriminating artistic eye of the antique collector just as easily as it does the hoarder of brown paper and string!

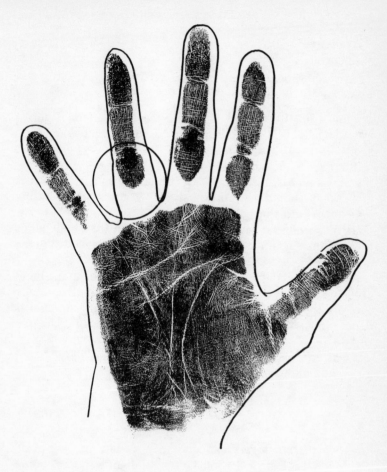

Print 6. *Full Basal Phalanx on the Ring Finger*

MERCURY OR THE LITTLE FINGER

Mythologically, Mercury was the messenger of the gods and giver of sleep. Because of his classical role the finger of Mercury has now come to represent:

- communcations
- literary talents

39

- business
- finance
- medicine
- science
- self-expression
- one's sexual and subconscious drives

A long, lean little finger is usually seen on anyone who is articulate, who is a good speaker or orator and who has a keen and ready wit. Literary types, writers, poets and those in the media often have long Mercury fingers. A short finger denotes shyness, reticence and diffidence, and the Mercury finger may sometimes *appear* short because it is set rather low down into the palm (see Print 7). Such a finger is the mark of a profound lack of self-confidence. A tip which bends towards the ring finger denotes the self-sacrificing spirit of the altruist.

A long top phalanx on the Mercury finger is seen in the hand of the charmer, the person who has the gift of the gab and who can talk the hind legs off a donkey. Long middle phalanges denote those in the caring or vocational professions, doctors and nurses for example, although some scientists may possess this feature too. Finally, long basal phalanges may show a need for mental and physical freedom.

THE FINGERTIPS

The tips of the fingers can end in a variety of shapes as illustrated in Figure 8. Some are blunt and square, some are conic or spatulate, and others are pointed. Each shape is associated with distinctive characteristics.

- *Square-tipped fingers* Add a practical, pragmatic and earthy quality.
- *Conic-tipped fingers* Facilitate the easy interchange of ideas and communications.
- *Spatulate-tipped fingers* Implement innovative, far-reaching ideas.
- *Pointed fingers* Enable quick reactions and responses. On a

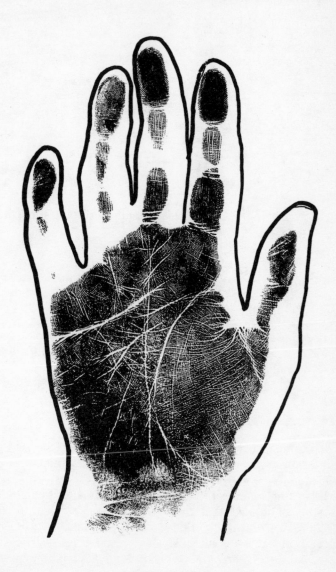

Print 7. Low-set Mercury Finger

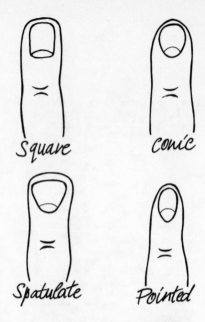

Figure 8. The Fingertips

negative hand this can lead to a sense of being 'too clever by half', to bitchiness or underhanded and downright manipulative behaviour.

FINGER SETTINGS

The normal setting for fingers into the palm is in the form of a gentle curve. This shows a well-balanced individual, someone with moderate views and a tolerant outlook.

If the fingers are set in a straight, even line, self-confidence is so pronounced that there is a danger of their owners becoming arrogant Figure 9a. Such people have plenty of drive and can be a bit pushy and sometimes even aggressive. Because there are few self-doubts, people with this straight setting generally believe that whatever they do must be right!

Very low-set indices (Figure 9b) suggest a 'chip on the shoulder', usually caused by an inferiority complex.

When only the little finger is noticeably low-set as in Figure 9c, it reveals a fundamental lack of self-confidence, often instilled at an early age through environmental or parental conditioning. Perhaps the child strongly felt that she failed to meet her parents' expectations; or felt unable to compete

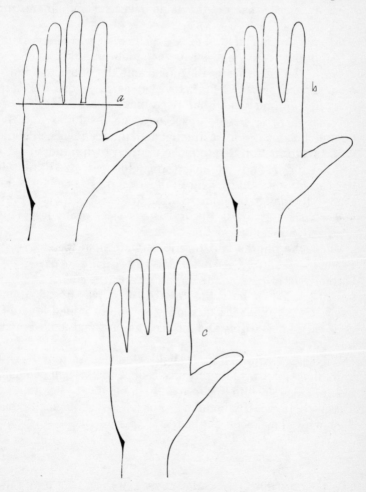

Figure 9. Finger Settings

with brighter, cleverer or more attractive brothers and sisters; or simply that she didn't fit in with her family philosophy or background.

FINGER SPACINGS

How the fingers fall in relation to each other when the hand is placed flat on the table reveals some interesting insights.

All the fingers held tightly together suggest a reserved, possibly introverted and fairly dependent individual.

When the fingers are all spread out the subject is fairly open and extroverted. This is the sign of a vivacious and alert, outgoing, optimistic and happy-go-lucky nature.

When there is a wide space between the index and the second fingers it shows intellectual independence. People with this formation like to make up their own minds.

If the middle and ring fingers are held apart, (see Print 8) it indicates resourcefulness. In adults it denotes a need for some time in the day to be alone in order to 'recharge the batteries' and refresh their minds. In children it's a sign of shyness. This is a fairly unusual formation.

When the middle and ring fingers are held together, (see Print 9) it shows a need for security. Domestic peace and harmony is of paramount importance to the owners of this formation. When only the tips of these two fingers point towards each other it can show a sense of divided loyalties between domestic duty and the need for personal achievement in a career.

Whenever the little finger is held widely apart from the rest it highlights the need for physical independence and personal freedom. People with this formation immediately feel trapped if they are physically hemmed in or feel psychologically that their wings have been clipped.

FINGER WIDTHS

The broader the fingers, the more self-assurance and self-confidence they portray. People with broad digits are often open-minded, tolerant, fair, generous and helpful. Very thin fingers can denote extreme austerity and may even suggest narrow-mindedness, cynicism and a mordantly critical mentality.

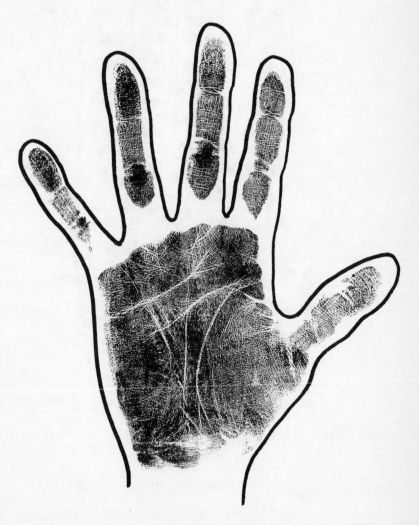

Print 8. Middle Fingers Held Apart

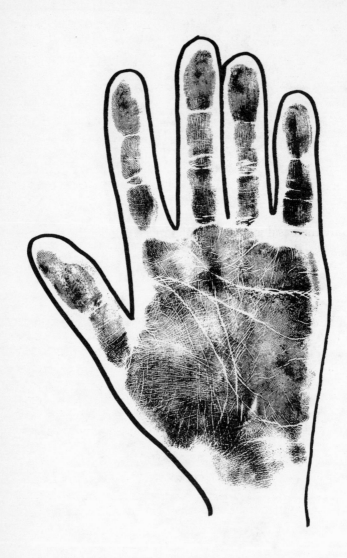

Print 9. Middle Fingers Held Together

FINGER JOINTS

Some people have very smooth fingers, whilst others have noticeably protruberant joints. Smooth-fingered folk are generally of the inspirational kind, as their ideas come and go almost without needing any processing, and because of this they can be categorized as impressionable.

When both the top and bottom joints are pronounced these are known as 'knotted fingers', and imply a philosophical turn of mind. Such people need to take time to think things out, especially when they are faced with making decisions or when they have a problem to sort out. Never expect these people to respond instantly; they really do need time to reflect, to consider and to analyze their thoughts before formulating their answers.

If only the basal joints are pronounced, whilst the top ones are smooth, it reveals a person who needs a tidy and ordered environment in which to live and work.

THE THUMB

The thumb is a uniquely human development and provides much insight into character and personality. Ideally, this digit should look balanced and in harmony with the rest of the hand. It represents will-power and drive together with reason and logic. Too small, weak or thin in comparison to the rest and the individual lacks strength of character. Over-large, heavy or bulbous in relation to the fingers and palm would denote someone who is perhaps forceful, over-dominant and aggressive.

Like the fingers, the thumb is make up of three phalanges. The top one reveals the individual's will-power; the middle phalanx denotes logic and reasoning; the basal phalanx is actually embedded in the palm, and forms the Mount of Venus.

LENGTHS

The length of the thumb should balance the palm and fingers. A good rule is that the nail phalanx should be longer than any single phalanx on any of the other fingers.

Short thumbs show a lack of reasoning and logical powers. People with this feature tend to work instinctively, and may feel that they lack control over the events in their lives, and that they are at the mercy of prevailing circumstances. This is especially so if the thumb is both short and weak.

Short, thick thumbs illustrate a lack of sensitivity and possible tendencies to cruelty. A bulbous thumb is the sign of aggression and ruthlessness; it is the mark of the tyrant and the despot.

A long thumb denotes excellent rational powers. If it is also aesthetically well-shaped, it indicates elegance and refinement of thought and ideas.

STIFFNESS VS SUPPLENESS

Some thumbs are stiff, some are supple and others are so flexible that they are known as double-jointed (Figure 10).

Stiff thumbs, as in Figure 10a, are associated with:

- inflexibility of character
- reserved, strong-willed nature
- playing one's cards close to one's chest
- closed personality with masses of self-control
- cool and clinical
- dogged, determined and persistent
- rigid in outlook

Supple thumbs, as in Figure 10b, denote:

- flexibility
- adaptability
- easy-going nature
- able to flow with the tide
- open
- tolerant and broad-minded
- quick learner

Flexible only at the top joint, as in Figure 10c, suggests:

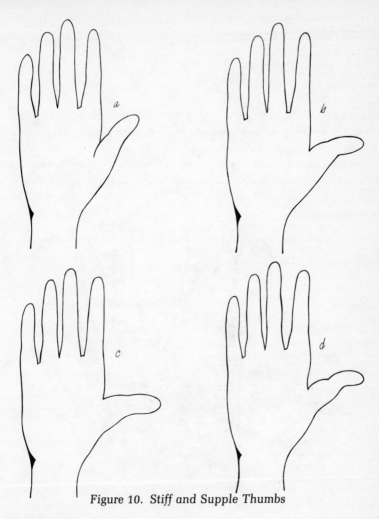

Figure 10. *Stiff and Supple Thumbs*

- inconsistency
- mental agility
- ability to switch from one activity to another

A double-jointed thumb, as in Figure 10d, reveals:

- character weaknesses
- easily distracted

49

- easily influenced
- tendency to give in too quickly

ANGLE OF OPENING

Oriental hand analysts maintain that a thumb that opens out to 90 degrees shows harmony of mind, body and spirit. The norm, though, is for the thumb to form an angle of between 45 and 90 degrees (see Print 10), where it denotes a confident, easy-going, sunny disposition, a good blend

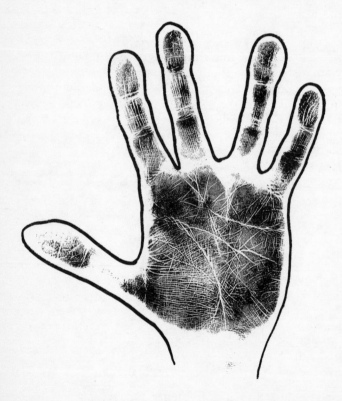

Print 10. 45–90 Degree Angle of the Opening of the Thumb

of introversion/extroversion and a generally well-balanced mentality.

An angle of more than 90 degrees reveals the extrovert or the exhibitionist. These people are non-conformist, often adventurous and possibly too open for their own good. They lack concentration and are all too easily distracted. What's more, this is the sign of extravagance. Never send these people out shopping with an open cheque book and without a specific shopping list!

A thumb which forms an angle of less than 45 degrees highlights a more introverted and inhibited nature. These people are persistent and able to concentrate for long periods at a time. They tend to be reserved, keeping themselves to themselves. The tighter the angle, the more intense, controlled and self-restrained the individual. Narrow-mindedness and bigotry are associated with a narrow angle of opening.

Sometimes a thumb held at a very acute angle reveals that the individual is going through a difficult time. It points to a need for added concentration and great self-control while he or she is mustering his or her resources and reappraising the situation. As the problems are resolved the thumb will begin to adopt a more relaxed pose.

There may be discrepancies in the angle of opening between the right and left hands. If, on a right-hander, the right thumb doesn't open as widely as the left it illustrates *either* a temporary crisis *or* that hard times have forced the individual to somehow conform or to impose tighter controls on herself. If it's the right thumb that forms the wider angle, it would show that the individual's childhood – either because of financial difficulties, sickness, bigoted parents, or whatever – was restrictive and it wasn't until that person matured and found her own independence that she was able to fully develop her own personality.

THUMB SETTINGS

In general, a thumb set high on the hand seems to form a much more acute angle to the palm than one which is set lower down (Figure 11). It would seem fair to assume, then,

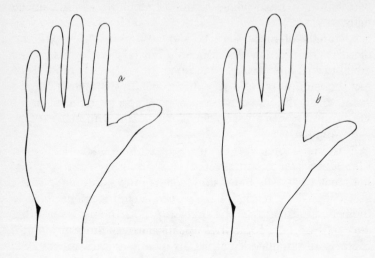

Figure 11. Thumb Settings

that a high-set thumb (figure 11a) denotes a more introverted and introspective person, whilst the lower the setting (figure 11b) the more extroverted and expansive the individual.

THE NAIL OR TOP PHALANX

This section of the thumb represents will-power. The shorter the phalanx, the less strength of will is implied; the longer, the more determination and will-power exists.

A broad section shows the power of leadership. Its owner is the sort of person who can pitch in with the rest without ever losing that position of control or command. If the section is long and lean it is again the sign of the leader, but this time it's more representative of the theoretical or academic type of person. Those who have slender top phalanges here are able to get what they want out of life with tremendous grace and charm. If full and padded, this section tells of an even temperament, an unflappable and steady sort of person.

A squared-off tip to the thumb conveys a practical, reliable and sensible disposition. A conic tip shows those who, although graceful in their approach, can easily become deflected from their goals and objectives in life. When this digit is spatulate it is known as the 'potter's thumb', and highlights the craftsman, someone who is manually skilled, sensitive and creative with his or her hands. If the top phalanx is pointed it can denote a nervous disposition, one who works in fits and starts.

THE SECOND PHALANX

This is the section which deals with reason and logic. If it is very short in comparison to the top section it tells that action will be instinctive and spontaneous rather than logically worked out. When it's of a good length it displays reasoned action. People with this formation admire articulacy, rhetoric and oratory. They are the ones who enjoy discussion

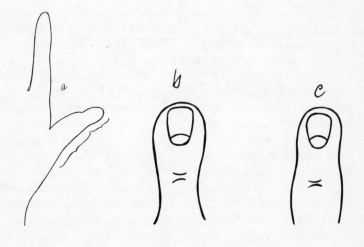

Figure 12. The Second Phalanx

and debate so much that they often stay up talking well into the early hours.

If the second phalanx is much longer than the top section (Figure 12a) it reveals those who *think* more than they *do*. These are the people who over-rationalize; they analyze everything, working out all the pros and cons, so much so that they tire themselves out long before they are able to put any of their good ideas into action. Too much logic and not enough determination characterizes this formation, and its owners have difficulty in realizing their ambitions.

When the second phalanx is waisted like an hour-glass (Figure 12b) it denotes the tactician, the person who is always discreet and knows how to deal with others in a diplomatic fashion. Overly thick, though, and it tells of one who is blunt and to the point (Figure 12c), who tends to see tact as simply evasiveness, and eloquent language as a means of masking indecision.

THE THREE ANGLES OF THE THUMB

If the top joint of the thumb is markedly pronounced it denotes stubbornness even to the point of bloody-mindedness (Figure 13a). A pronounced basal joint (Figure 13b) is known as the angle of manual dexterity. It reveals nimble fingers and is invariably found on those who are good at handicrafts, DIY, playing musical instruments or anything requiring dexterous fingerwork.

If the palm sweeps out into a sharp, well-defined angle at the wrist, it is known as the angle of rhythm and timing (Figure 13c). This development is found on the hands of those who have a good ear for music, and who often play a musical instrument. It also denotes a keen sense of timing such as possessed by good sportsmen or comedians. Otherwise, it may simply reveal a strict feel for punctuality.

THE NAILS

The shape of the nails (Figure 14) provides a rich source of information about an individual's character and behaviour.

Figure 13. The Three Angles of the Thumb

- large, squarish nails reveal a placid nature, someone who is slow to anger
- smaller square nails suggest a cynical and critical view of life
- oblong nails, wider than they are high, reveal a very quick temper. (This may be slow to show itself, but when it does it explodes with volcanic force! This type of nail is usually only found on the thumb)
- long, filbert-shaped nails denote an even temper and a good nature
- short, rounded nails often indicate quick, intuitive powers
- almond-shaped nails tell of a gentle, easy-going nature; such people tend to be refined, and also have a sensitive disposition
- fan-shaped nails indicate a nervous, highly-strung individual

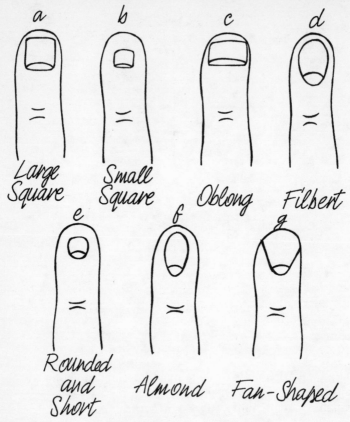

Figure 14. The Shape of the Nails

MOONS

The size and appearance of the moons reveal aspects about the individual's health.

- large moons are associated with a strong heart and good circulation
- small, even moons depict overall sound health
- no moons suggest poor circulation

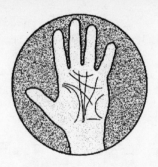

5 · FINGERPRINT PATTERNS

Our fingerprints are our very own personal signatures for they are totally unique. No two patterns are ever exactly alike, not even on the hands of identical twins. Unlike other features in the hand, our fingerprints never change their patterns throughout our lives. They are our individual identification marks.

These patterns can also be found on the palm and on the soles of our feet. On the hands they are known as palmar patterns, and on the feet they are called plantar patterns. The modern scientific name for the study of skin patterning is dermatoglyphics. The term is derived from the two Classical words: *derma*, meaning skin, and *glyph*, which means a carving. So, literally, dermatoglyphics stands for the study of the skin carvings: those tiny ridges or furrows that form themselves into the familiar patterns on our hands and feet.

ORIGINS

Early in the nineteenth century Dr Jan Evangelista, a young Czechoslovakian physician, first identified skin patterns whilst working on the spiral sweat glands in the hand. Further interest in the subject we now call dermatoglyphics was aroused when more discoveries were made towards the end of that century. In the latter half of the nineteenth century. came the news from Japan that a medical missionary, Dr Henry Faulds, had excavated fragments of ancient pottery bearing thumb prints which had been pressed into the base of each pot. Faulds deduced, quite correctly, that the marks had been used as the potter's signature, and that therefore implied that each individual's thumb print is unique. This conclusion was supported by a Commissioner of Police in India, who observed that it was the custom for illiterate Indians to press their thumb prints onto official documents to stand as their personal signatures.

Back in England Francis Galton who, having heard of these findings, became the true pioneer of fingerprinting as we know it today. Throughout his lifetime he collected and classified thousands of specimens and proved categorically the uniqueness and individuality of skin patterns. It was through his work that fingerprinting became universally accepted and used in criminal investigation and identification.

Today, modern hand analysts not only recognize the different patterns but, through observation and deduction, they have also attached character and personality traits to them. A lot of exciting new research is currently being carried out in the medical field too, which is establishing a link between certain skin patterns and congenital or hereditary conditions such as Down's Syndrome, hypertension and susceptibility to heart disease. This research suggests that any chromosomal or congenital abnormalities that are part of an individual's genetic blueprint stamp themselves in the form of specific markings into the skin patterns of the hands around the third month of foetal development.

FINGERPRINTS

There are three basic categories of fingerprints: the loop, the whorl and the arch. These three then subdivide further, as shown in Figure 15, to form several other variations or configurations which bring the number of patterns to about six or seven different identifiable types.

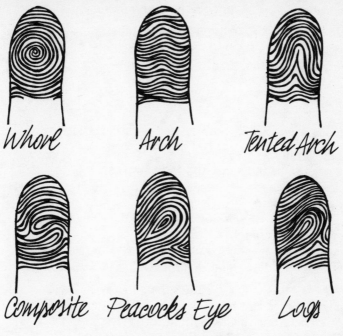

Figure 15. Fingerprint Patterns

Some people have a complete set of one particular pattern on all ten digits. Others may have one pattern on one hand, and a completely different one on the other. Still others may have a combination of patterns; two or three whorls, let's say, a couple of arches and the rest as loops. In such cases each pattern must be interpreted according the individual finger.

LOOPS

The most common fingerprint pattern is the loop. It denotes:

- flexibility
- adaptability
- a love of communications and new ideas
- a dislike of routine
- a need for a buzzing work and home life
- a love of different interests

- excellent abilities in working with other people

A loop on any individual finger would indicate a flexible and free-and-easy attitude in whatever sphere of influence is represented by that digit.

WHORLS

The key characteristics associated with the whorl are:

- inflexibility
- a need to be in charge and in control
- deep thinkers
- dogmatic views
- a preference for working for and by themselves
- creative turn of mind
- slowness in making up one's mind and in responding
- a need for time to consider, reflect and process information

On the index, the whorl shows that at work its owners prefer to be in charge and hate others constantly looking over their shoulders telling them what to do.

On the ring finger, the whorl is an indicator of artistic or creative potential.

On the little finger, the whorl highlights the quiet retiring types. These people are not idle chatterers but prefer to talk on matters they know and understand well. However, once they embark on their favourite subject, it's almost impossible to stop them!

On the thumb, the whorl especially denotes the slow types, those who are entrenched in their ideas and have particular difficulty in changing their attitudes and opinions. This strong pattern on a strong thumb reveals someone who likes to be the boss.

ARCHES

Arches are linked with:

- practicality
- down-to-earth mentality

- salt-of-the-earth character
- reliability
- trustworthiness
- plenty of common sense
- difficulty in verbally expressing feelings
- conversation centres around concrete, everyday, material subjects

Arches on the index and middle fingers especially highlight an inability to express verbally personal emotions. These people must find a practical outlet – painting, pottery, writing, knitting, sewing, and so on – through which to express themselves, otherwise they might be in danger of repressing their feelings altogether. On the thumbs, arches denote those whose feet are firmly planted on the ground and who are excellent at giving good, sound, practical advice.

A full set of arches needs to be investigated thoroughly as this can, in some cases, indicate the possibility of chromosomal complications.

TENTED ARCHES

The tented arch is usually found only on the index. It is associated with:

- single-mindedness
- a need for an impetus or a challenge in life
- working in bouts of enthusiasm
- sudden obsessions
- tendency to follow cults/religions/ideologies
- seekers after truth

COMPOSITES

The composite looks like two loops pulling in opposite directions, rather like the yin/yang symbol. People who possess this pattern are described as:

- having the ability to see all sides of a problem
- tendency to spend too long weighing up the pros and cons
- indecisive

- argumentative
- questioning

The composite is usually found only on the index and thumb, and in these positions it bodes well for judges, lawyers, counsellors or anyone who needs to understand or appreciate another person's point of view. But, at the same time, this pattern can denote conflicting drives, confusion and difficulty when it comes to making important decisions that affect the personal lives of the individuals themselves.

THE PEACOCK'S EYE

This pattern consists of a whorl inside a loop and looks, as its name implies, like the 'eye' on the tail feather of a peacock. It is usually found only on the ring or little fingers and those who have it are blessed with:

- protection
- good fortune
- experience of lucky escapes from injurious or dangerous situations

PALMAR PATTERNS

Similar patterns to those on the finger tips can also occur elsewhere on the hand. Loops may be found on the palm between the fingers, and other patterns are sometimes seen on the Mount of Venus (Figure 16). On the Mount of Luna the patterns may take a variety of forms and may lie in several different directions across the area.

- *Between the thumb and index finger* A courageous spirit.
- *Between the index and second fingers* Executive ability. Often found in the hands of people in professional occupations.
- *Between the second and third fingers* A vocational spirit. People with this marking have a fundamental need to work for the community or for the good of others.
- *Between the third and fourth fingers* A rather dry and odd sense of humour.

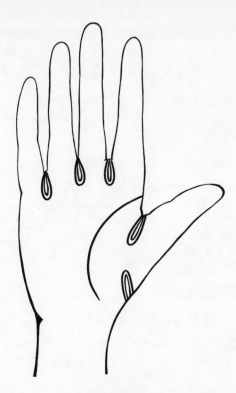

Figure 16. Palmar Loops

- On the *Mount of* Venus Markings in this area denote musical talents.
- *The Mount of Luna* This is an area which can be rich in loops, whorls or composites (Figure 17).

A *loop lying across this mount* (Figure 17a) denotes a love of Nature, an understanding of and a rapport with flora and/or fauna.

A *curved loop below the Head line* (Figure 17b) reveals an affinity to water. There is invariably some kind of connection with rivers or the sea either in terms of location or sporting interests or, simply, that the subject feels drawn to water and is in turn invigorated, refreshed, inspired or soothed by it.

A *loop rising upwards from the wrist* (Figure 17c) is the

63

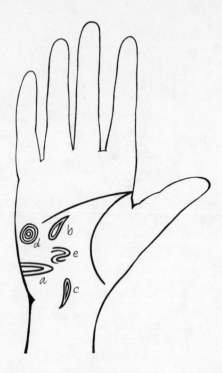

Figure 17. *Palmar Patterns on the Mount of Luna*

mark of inspiration, that delicate and ethereal stuff that poets and painters are blessed with.

A *whorl* (Figure 17d) in this area often suggests a special gift or talent. Sometimes, those who possess this marking feel a great longing to fulfil themselves either creatively or through commitment and service to humanity.

A *composite pattern* (Figure 17e) here would indicate personal uncertainty or indecision regarding the individual's own gifts and talents.

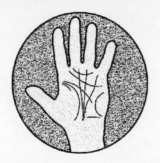

6 · THE MAJOR LINES

A glance at the tiny hands of a new-born baby will not only show that babies are born with their lines already formed, but also that those lines stand out clearly in the palm. Because the major lines in the hands are formed in the embryo some time around the third month of foetal development, every baby comes into the world already equipped with his or her unique set of markings.

From then on, lines can and do change throughout the individual's life according to experiences, decisions, changes of lifestyle, states of health or whatever events occur which may modify that person's self-awareness or understanding of his or her environment. Lines may be added, strengthened, weakened, lengthened, may deteriorate or, in some extreme cases, fade away altogether.

Each line represents a particular aspect of an individual's life and it is the quality, appearance and construction of the line that gives clues to its owner's character, and to the events that are likely to happen in the course of his or her life. The four main creases in the hand which reflect these aspects are known as the Head, Life, Heart and Fate lines (Figure 18). Figure 19 illustrates the type of markings that may be found on or across these lines.

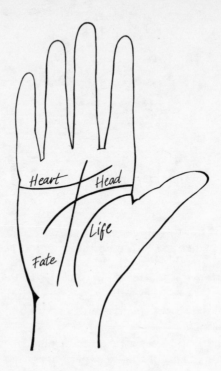

Figure 18. The Major Lines

THE HEAD LINE

The Head line represents our:

- intellectual potential
- mental stance
- outlook on life

A good, strong Head line holds the power to overcome almost any other physical, psychological or emotional problem that may be seen elsewhere on the hand.

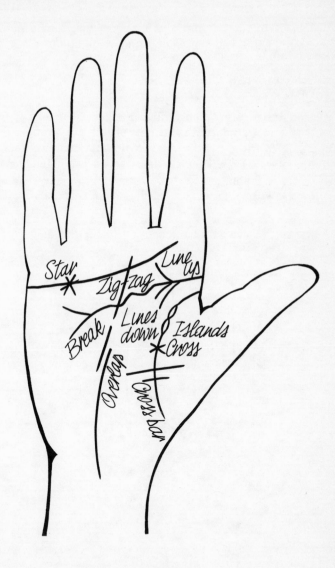

Figure 19. Types of Markings on the Hand

POSITION

The line begins at the palm edge just above the thumb and travels across the palm. It is the second transverse line in the hand.

QUALITY

A Head line is considered strong when it is clear, unbroken and well-etched. People with this sort of line are strong-minded, positive, forthright individuals who find making decisions comparatively easy. They are decisive, clear-sighted and intellectually independent.

But if the line is faint, broken, chained or islanded (Figure 20),

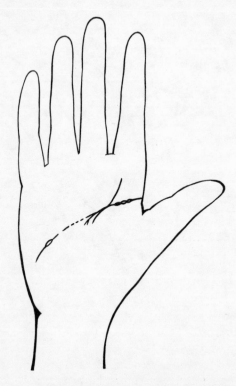

Figure 20. A Weak Head Line

it is considered weak. Owners of such a line would find decision-making particularly difficult. Perhaps they might be plagued with worry and anxiety of one sort or another and they might, at times, lack concentration and clarity of thought.

It's possible to find Head lines that are strong in places and weaker in others. This sort of line reveals phases of mental alertness and activity interspersed with periods of indecisiveness and 'cotton-wool' thinking.

DIRECTION

There are two fundamental types of Head lines: one which travels in a straight line across the palm, and another which is curved.

A straight Head line (Figure 21a) indicates a practical, pragmatic mentality and a convergent thinker. Such people have a fairly materialistic outlook and they normally take a rational, concrete, down-to-earth approach to life. If they are academically minded they would favour scientific or technological subjects; business and commerce would suit them too.

A Head line that curves gently downwards (Figure 21b) reveals the more creative or artistically minded person, the divergent thinker. Such folk are found in the humanities; anything connected with communications, languages, design, arts and crafts and dealing with other people would be suitable.

A Head line that is part straight and part curved reveals a combination of the practical and creative mentality. These are the people who can enjoy the arts as well as the sciences and, because of this, they find it difficult to decide which they prefer. The best advice is for owners of the combination line to think about the more applied subjects, the softer sciences or anything which combines structure with creative flair. If they are in a scientific or an out-and-out practical type of job they should try to cultivate some creative hobbies. Alternatively, those who find themselves in purely artistic occupations ought to think about a more practical pastime in order to balance out their interests.

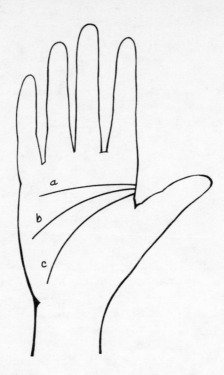

Figure 21. Direction of the Head Line

A steeply curved line ending low down on the Mount of Luna (Figure 21c) reveals tremendous imagination which, if unrestrained, can lead to melancholia and depression. In extreme cases, these people can be so creative that, at times, they may be in danger of teetering on that brink between genius and madness. Certainly, these are the types whose moods can easily swing up or down and so may be clinically manic depressive. Generally, they tend to work in spurts: greatly enthusiastic one minute, and fed up the next. The best advice for them is to try to harness their energy and to channel their moods into creative output. This is the only way their rich imagination and artistic talents will be able to develop and flower.

The Simian line (see Print 11) is a fairly unusual feature in a normal hand. It is formed when the two lines of Head and Heart are fused together into one single line, lying right across the palm from edge to edge. Although the Simian line is one of the most recognizable signs of Down's Syndrome, it does occur in about 6 per cent of normal hands.

This line is the mark of intensity. People with a Simian line have the ability to concentrate and to channel their thinking, and they are often described as single-minded. They tend to compartmentalize every facet of their lives so that when they are concentrating on their work, for example, they can only think about the job in hand. When they concentrate on a hobby they switch off all else and focus solely on that. It's almost as if they can pull the shutters down in order to dedicate themselves to the particular task at that moment in time.

On the emotional side, this intensity can manifest itself in jealousy. They believe that as they give themselves totally to the ones they love, they expect their love to be reciprocated to the exclusion of all others and all else. If the Simian line has both the tails of the Heart and Head lines projecting from it, rather than being one single line, the intensity is eased and the jealousy mellows with increasing age and experience.

LENGTH

The actual length of the Head line can give some important insights into the scope and intellectual potential of the individual.

A short line, that is, one that ends under the middle finger, reveals a somewhat earthy and mundane mentality. Those who possess such a line seem to be more concerned with material security than others and their conversations generally run along concrete lines; they prefer to talk about cars, holidays, houses, clothes, money, and so on, rather than abstract concepts.

A long Head line, one which runs past the base of the ring finger, shows a keen intelligence and an aptitude for abstract

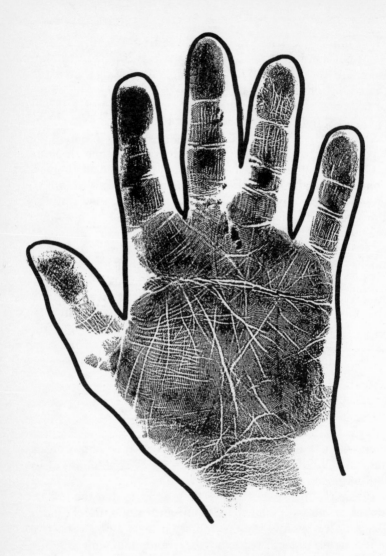

Print 11. The Simian Line

thought – just as long, of course, as it is of sound construction. This sort of line promises excellent prospects for successful intellectual abilities.

The next step is to minutely scrutinize the line along its course. This will provide an astonishing amount of psychological detail and insight into the character of the individual and the events surrounding his or her life.

Beginnings

When the Head line begins attached to the Life line (Figure 22a) it reveals a cautious, careful nature. Often, this can also show a closeness to the parental influences and early environment. If the lines are united for a considerable distance (Figure 22b), not separating until passing under the middle finger, it tells that the subject is a late developer, probably not becoming truly independent until much later than average.

If the Head line actually begins *inside* the Life line (Figure 22c), it points to someone who is insecure, self-conscious and possibly even lacking in self-confidence. As a consequence, this type may become aggressively defensive through life.

A good blend of caution and impulsiveness is seen in the hand where the two lines detach themselves quite early on, or where a small gap is seen between the two (Figure 22d). This is also a mark of self-confidence.

When the two lines are widely apart the individual is the adventurous, reckless and impulsive type. People with this formation are extremely independent, and show it at a very early age; invariably they are dare-devils, and the young girls will be tomboys. 'Live now, pay later' seems to be their attitude.

The higher up the palm and the closer to the fingers the Head line begins, the more ambitious the nature. These people are the cerebral types, highly achievement-motivated and with

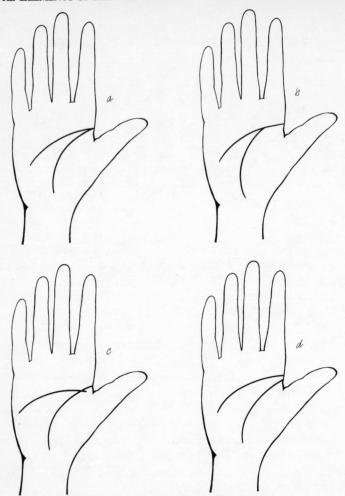

Figure 22. The Beginnings of the Head Line

plenty of drive to attain their goals and expectations in life. Generally, they don't let their emotions interfere with their rational processes; it's very much a case of their 'heads ruling their hearts'.

If, at its beginning, the Head line appears intricately interwoven or intermeshed with the Life line, or if it is islanded or chained (see Print 12), one of two interpretations may

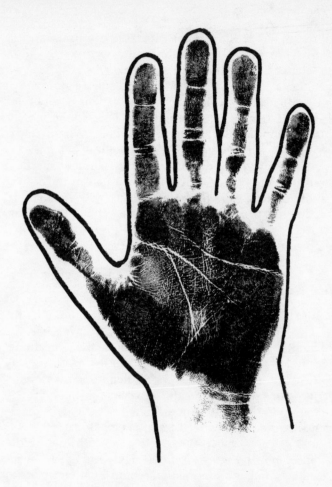

Print 12. Chained Beginning to the Head Line

apply. The line may be suggesting that its owner suffered a good deal with bronchial or respiratory problems as a child. Alternatively, the individual experienced early worries and anxieties, perhaps not feeling in tune with his or her parental or childhood environment. Other factors in the hand should help to distinguish which of these alternatives is applicable.

The Point of Separation

Careful examination of the point where the two lines separate reveals the process of maturation and how the individual actually achieves independence.

If the attached Head line lifts itself up and away from the Life line quite near its beginning, the subject has bodily lifted herself out of her early environment. This could happen through academic achievement, for example. When islands or crossing bars are present at the very point of separation it suggests that achieving independence was traumatic. Perhaps interference or opposition may have been placed in the way of the individual's desire for independence and freedom.

If the two lines separate cleanly and neatly, the transition from childhood to independent maturity occurs easily and harmoniously, with no major upheavals.

The First Half of the Head Line

As the line travels beneath the index finger it represents the early years of life, from birth to about twenty. This is where the developmental years, the parental influences, the educational progress and, finally, the maturation process is seen. Any islands (Figure 19) during this period denote worries, emotional upsets or possible ill health. Any branches (Figure 19) seen rising up to the index mount from here usually indicate academic achievements or feelings of personal success.

The next stage of the line, travelling beneath the middle finger, represents the early twenties right through to about forty. Again, islands on this section would highlight worries that last for the duration of the island itself. Any change in the structure or composition must be noted. Should the line strengthen, the thinking processes improve and the individual gains a more positive outlook. But if the line weakens or deteriorates in any way, indecision and a lack of both clarity of thought and of concentration have set in.

Sometimes the Head line may appear to zig-zag up and down (Figure 19). Even if only slightly noticeable, this represents peaks and troughs in the subject's intellectual progress through life. The peaks indicate periods when thinking is clear, channelled and unhampered. The troughs denote times of possible depression, when intellectually the individual is at a low ebb. Any dip in the line, or any downward pointing branch, no matter how tiny, will highlight times of 'low' when the subject is experiencing emotional problems and feeling generally depressed (Figure 19).

Conversely, any rising branch represents mental achievement. Branches rising towards the index finger usually indicate academic success. Those leading towards the Saturn finger show career prospects and achievements; towards the ring finger they highlight feelings of creative fulfilment and satisfaction; and branches towards the little finger show either scientific or business success, or possibly even financial gain.

A break with overlapping ends along any part of the Head line (Figure 19) is most interesting as it represents a complete change of awareness, a reorientation, often a completely new way of looking at life. People with this feature seem to undergo a whole process of change because of their experiences. Through this time they question their ideals, their long-held beliefs; they challenge their values and reassess their objectives and ambitions. In this way they emerge with a totally different outlook on life, which is then reflected by the position and quality of the new section of line.

If the new overlapping line lies above the old one, thus closer to the Heart line, the individual emerges more practically minded, more business-conscious, possibly a little harder but much more in control than before. If the new section commences underneath the old one, the individual becomes more relaxed, more expansive and perhaps much more open and creative.

A clean break, with no overlapping ends, is an unusual feature and could possibly denote an injury to the head, or a remarkable event which would end one part of the individual's life quite dramatically before opening up another.

Crossbars cutting the main line at any point represent times of interference, opposition or setbacks which temporarily impede the natural flow, and hamper the progress of the individual. If, after the obstruction, the line continues as normal, the interference has no long-lasting detrimental effects. Any damage from such events would be represented by islands or a weakening of the line itself.

The Second Half of the Head Line

As the Head line travels across the palm below the Apollo finger it relates roughly to the age of forty onwards. If the line is short it does not in any way infer a short life, but simply that the time scale may need to be compressed. It could also mean that the rest of the line has yet to be developed, and may well do so in the course of time.

The same rules apply to this part of the line as to the first half. Note the structure, and whether any changes, either of a positive or negative nature, occur. Are there any noticeable islands, bars or breaks which would suggest worry, opposition, interference or change? If downward branches are seen, these would indicate periods of depression. Rising branches, though, denote times of achievement.

On this section it is quite unusual to see branches shooting off to the index or middle finger mounts but, if they do exist, they would be interpreted as academic and career success. More usually, if there are rising branches, they would point towards the ring and little fingers. Those towards the ring finger suggest personal and creative fulfilment and satisfaction; to the little finger, scientific, commercial, technological or financial achievement.

Endings

If the line thins out towards the end it shows that there is more potential there, but that the mind is not being stretched to the full. The stronger the line at its termination, the more vigorous and alert the mind remains. When a line is tasselled, split or frayed at the end it can denote forgetfulness in old age and a general dissipation of mental energy. This can be one of the signs of senility.

In some cases, the Head line splits into a fork (Figure 19), but this must not be confused with the Fate line which rises up and cuts through the line. Nor should it be interpreted as a depression marking. When the line forks under the middle finger it may denote a talent for music, or alternatively an aptitude for anything to do with property and the land. Forking beneath the ring finger is rather special and is known as the 'writer's fork'. Not all writers have this mark nor, indeed, do all who possess it become writers. What it does show, however, is excellent creative or artistic talent. If the line forks below the little finger it highlights business, commercial or financial expertise.

DISCREPANCIES BETWEEN THE RIGHT AND THE LEFT HEAD LINES

Hand-reading becomes a fascinating study when differences are detected between the two hands, as this reveals the richness of character and complexities of the individual. Remember that on a right-handed person, the right hand portrays the objective side, whilst the left illustrates the subjective and, of course, vice versa for a left-hander.

Should the objective hand display a stronger Head line than the other, whether in terms of length or structure or composition, it reveals that such individuals have made more of their intellectual development than their inherited or early environmental background would have allowed.

If, however, it is the subjective hand which bears the stronger line, its owner has neither made the most of her intellectual capacity nor taken advantage of the opportunities presented to her in life. Should the Head line be forked at any point on the subjective hand alone it would suggest that the potential for expansion in those areas has not yet been developed.

THE LIFE LINE

The Life line represents our:

- vitality
- enthusiasm for living

79

- zest or verve for life
- state of health
- physical strength and robustness or weaknesses and frailties
- the general tenor of our lives

The fundamental mistake that so many people make with regard to this line is that they believe the Life line reveals the actual length of life itself. This is not so. The line represents the *quality*, not the *quantity*, of life.

POSITION

The Life line begins at the palm edge, usually half-way between the base of the index and the thumb. It may then form a wide sweep into the centre of the palm, or it can skirt tightly around the thumb.

When the line is seen to hug the Mount of Venus, keeping close to the thumb, it illustrates a lack of vital energy and a general lack of physical robustness. This is also a sign of emotional coolness and a certain personal reserve.

The further the line sweeps towards the centre of the palm the more outward-looking the individual. These people are generally virile and active, with plenty of stamina and vitality. They have a great enthusiasm for living life to the full and they seem to exude human warmth and charisma.

BEGINNINGS

The beginnings of the Life line follow exactly the same principles as the Head line (Figures 22a, b, c & d). If these two lines begin attached, it denotes a cautious, self-restrained individual. Furthermore, if the lines remain attached for a long way, it is the sign of the late developer. When the lines begin attached but separate early on, or even if there is a slight gap between the two, there is a good balance of common sense and caution together with a spirited sense of fun and adventure. A wide gap between the two indicates impetuosity, the adventurous dare-devil type who enjoys taking risks.

The average starting point of this line is roughly half-way down the palm from the base of the index finger to the thumb. The higher up the palm the line commences the more ambitious and, possibly, even masterful the individual. Beginning low down towards the thumb reveals uncertainty and a lack of self-confidence.

ISLANDS

Islands (Figure 19) on the Life line reveal a weakening of the constitution, periods of ill health or simply a general lack of robustness lasting for as long as the island is present.

A single island, or a chain of islands, at the beginning of the line below the index finger indicate childhood or early adolescent illnesses. Invariably, this formation here represents the bronchial or catarrhal types of illnesses which affect the respiratory system. Islands slightly further down along the line often denote back trouble. This could simply infer a general weakness of the back or spine or, in some cases, actual damage or injury to the back itself. Still further down the line towards the wrist, an island would indicate any weakness or ill health mainly associated with old age.

Islands must be investigated in conjunction with other features in the hand in order to establish physiological weaknesses and to ascertain the exact nature of the illness implied.

BREAKS

There are two types of breaks which may be seen on this line: a complete, clean break, and one where the ends of the line overlap (Figure 19).

A clean break can denote an accident, or sudden ill health. If a square formation is seen over the break itself it marks some form of protection against the danger, a cushioning effect which acts as a buffer to the events and so bodes well for a speedy recovery. A break with overlapping ends indicates the development of a brand new section of Life line and, as such, represents a change in the way of life: new beginnings, new horizons or a move to a new environment. The wider the space between the overlap, the greater the change. If the new section of line begins inside the old, as shown in Figure 23a, it shows that the changes bring a narrowing, a cramping, of the new life as opposed to the old one. This might occur, for example, after an accident where the individual's health has weakened or, perhaps, after an unhappy move. But if the new section begins outside the old, that is towards the centre of the palm, the new life brings great improvement, wider horizons, more activity and a general feeling of expansion.

A word of caution here. Sometimes a Life line appears to be unusually short, and as such may give great anxiety to the individual concerned. Such a line does not necessarily indicate a short life. Many apparently short Life lines (as in Figure 23b) have a tiny hair-line joining them to a new line further out towards the centre of the palm or even, in some instances, to the Fate line itself. Rather than denoting an early death, this type of line reveals the beginning of a brand new

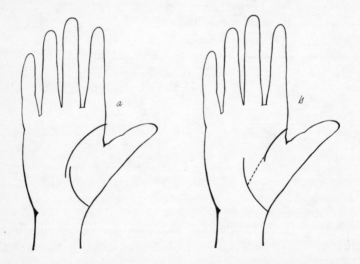

Figure 23. Breaks in the Life Line

life at the time indicated. For example, these people might emigrate, or marry, or move into quite a different world to the one they had been used to.

BRANCHES

There are two types of branches which come off the Life line: those which rise up towards the fingers, and those which drop down towards the wrist (Figure 19).

Rising branches are effort lines showing personal triumphs and a sense of accomplishment. Up towards the index mount a branch suggests academic endeavours. Towards the middle finger implies successes connected with property, with domestic stability or with occupational matters. A branch rising towards the ring finger highlights creative fulfilment and contentment. One rising towards the little finger reveals a sense of satisfaction in anything connected with scientific, literary, commercial or financial affairs.

Branches which drop downwards denote movement, either implying a change of address or journeys and travel in general. The shorter or finer the branch, the less impact the move has on the individual; the longer the branch, the more important or the further away is the relocation. A long branch often represents travels abroad, especially so if the branch penetrates deep into the Luna mount.

CROSS BARS

Bars that lie across the Life line (Figure 24a) are called trauma lines and indicate times of obstruction, opposition or interference, all of which create emotional upheaval or turmoil. The bolder the crossing line, the greater the upset. If the cross bar begins at the base of the thumb and travels over the main line, it suggests problems of a family or parental nature. When the cross bar cuts right through the Life line and then proceeds to cut through the Head and/or the Heart line, the trauma has significant repercussions throughout the individual's life.

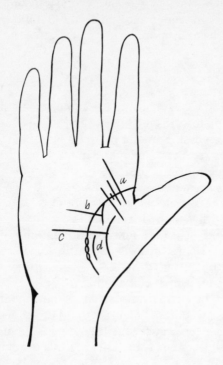

Figure 24. Markings on the Life Line

If there are many of these lines but they are fine and closely packed, rather than specific events they denote a highly strung, fretful nature and someone who is prone to worry. When a cross bar begins from an influence line inside the main Life line (Figure 24b) it tells that the problem stems from that relationship.

INFLUENCE LINES

These lines are seen on the inside of the Life line, either springing out from the main line itself or independently paralleling it (Figure 24c). Both may denote either children or new relationships. The quality of each line will reveal what sort of influence the relationship has upon the individual.

SISTER LINES

A sister line is a parallel line to the Life line which follows it around on the inside. This is also called the line of Mars and it has two interpretations. Firstly, it can represent a strong influence such as a close and loving soul mate or sometimes, even, a rich inner spiritual life. In other cases, this line suggests extra vitality and protection, rather like back-up reserves, especially so if the main Life line is broken, chained or islanded (Figure 24d). Such a line adds a boost to the vital strength and life energy.

THE HEART LINE

The Heart line relays information about our:

- emotions
- attitudes to love, marriage and relationships
- health
- mineral imbalances and general body chemistry

POSITION

The Heart line is the first transverse lying across the palm directly beneath the fingers. If it appears to lie considerably high up in the hand, so that it seems to be very close to the fingers, it reveals an intellectual approach to the emotions. These people are cool, rational, analytical: the sort whose head rules the heart. Lower down on the palm, so that it is displaced closer to the Head line, reveals that the emotions take precedence, and that, in fact, the heart rules the head.

If the line is very straight (Figure 25a), especially if this formation is seen on a female hand, it usually denotes a shrewd and sometimes even a calculative approach to human relationships. The straight Heart line has often been referred to as denoting 'masculine' emotions.

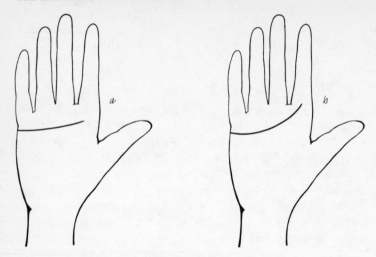

Figure 25. The Heart Line

Alternatively, when the line is deeply curved (Figure 25b) it highlights a generous, giving and sensitive approach to relationships. Whether this is seen on the male or female hand it is referred to as a 'feminine' line. Whenever it is seen, it also indicates a strong sense of justice, of mercy and of fair play; so strong, in fact, that people with this type of line invariably go to great pains to give others chance after chance to redeem or to explain themselves, and often end up getting kicked in the teeth for their trouble!

ENDINGS

The line which ends on the index mount (Figure 26a) indicates idealism in affairs of the heart. These people tend to have a rosy picture of relationships and marriage, seeing their lovers rather like knights in shining armour or fair damsels in distress. They have extremely high ideals and even higher standards of excellence. As a consequence, they are in danger of suffering disappointments and disillusionment when they discover that those they have placed on a pedestal are merely human and that, like everyone else, they have feet of clay.

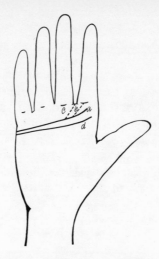

Figure 26. Heart Line Endings

When let down in this way, it takes them a long time to regain the love and trust they had invested; if, indeed, they ever do again. The best advice would be that they should try to lower their expectations, to be more realistic about relationships and about human nature in general.

If the line ends very high up on the index mount (Figure 26b), almost reaching the base of the finger, it can indicate jealousy and possessiveness not only of lovers and husbands but of children and friends too.

When the line is seen to end between the first and second fingers (Figure 26c), it shows a sensible, down-to-earth attitude to marital relationships. These people are warm-hearted but, because they find it difficult to express their inner feelings verbally, they prefer to show their love through the things they do for others. As this can result in repressing their emotions, they need some sort of safety-valve, either a friendly ear to listen to their problems, or perhaps they could record their feelings in a diary.

A line that ends under the middle finger denotes sensuality. These people are more interested in one-night stands and in their own sexual gratification than in emotional commitment.

Work rather than relationships takes priority for people who have a line which travels straight across the palm, beneath the index and almost to the palm edge (Figure 26d). All other aspects of life have to fit in accordingly, and their loved ones have to learn to give them the necessary space and time they need to pursue their careers. These are the people who, because of the devotion and dedication to their work, are often found on committees, or called upon time and again to shoulder responsibility.

A line which has three forks is considered to be the ideal as it encompasses all the categories described above: the warmth, the idealism, the passion and the sensible approach to all human relationships.

BRANCHES

Branches which drop downwards off the Heart line (see Figure 19), may represent times of emotional disappointments and unhappiness, especially so if they strike the Head line.

ISLANDS

Islands on this line are health indicators. Under the index/middle fingers an island may indicate hearing difficulties. Under the ring finger an island may denote potential sight defects, whilst a laddering effect here may also pinpoint nervousness, coupled with a possible disturbance in the sleep pattern, perhaps due to an imbalance of calcium. In general, a chained Heart line may indicate minor deficiencies or imbalances.

Any other markings on this line, such as breaks or dots, could be potential pointers to certain cardiac or vascular conditions but these must be verified by other indications or factors elsewhere in the hand.

THE FATE LINE

The Fate line represents our:

• public selves

- careers
- way of life
- sense of responsibility
- general awareness of ourselves, of our roles and standing in society

BEGINNINGS

This line can have several starting points but the normal rule is that the Fate line rises up the hand, usually through the centre of the palm, and travels towards the middle finger.

If it takes its roots from the Luna mount (Figure 27a) it reveals a career which involves being in the public eye or, better still, in the limelight. People with this line need public approval and recognition. Those who have a Fate line which begins attached to the Life line (Figure 27b) invariably experience early family responsibilities and commitments. A boy who takes over as head of the family due to the loss of the father, or a young daughter who feels it her duty to care for her sick parents, might both have this feature. It is not until the lines separate that the responsibilities change and the individuals feel free to pursue their independent lives.

When the line travels in a straight course right up the centre of the palm, it shows a steady, settled sort of existence, uninterrupted by any of life's major highs or lows. Due to increased mobility and today's unemployment situation, this sort of line is not seen quite as often nowadays as it used to be. It represents a predisposed path in life, such as might be seen on those who follow in their father's footsteps, or who are employed in the same firm from the time they leave school until they retire. This line also adds a touch of fatalism to the individual's philosophy of life.

The Fate line may begin higher up in the palm (Figure 27c), but it is not until it starts that it marks the beginning of a sense of control over the environment, the idea of responsibility and the feeling of purpose and commitment in life. In a few cases, the development of this line may indicate feelings of restriction but this would, of course, have to be analyzed according to the rest of the hand.

89

Figure 27. The Fate Line

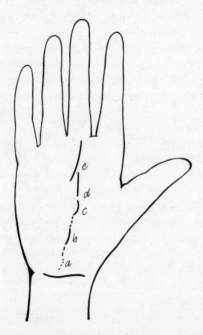

Figure 28. The Course of the Fate Line

THE COURSE OF THE LINE

If the line is faint or fragmented, especially at the beginning, it denotes vacillation, no firm ideas about the future, perhaps a lack of purpose or direction, and it also shows frequent changes of jobs (Figure 28a). Where the actual texture of the line is uneven, appearing thicker and then thinner (figure 28b) it tells of the varying degrees of control the individuals feel they have over their lives; sometimes they feel in command and then, at other times, they may feel at the mercy of their circumstances.

Any breaks, or even the slightest deviation in the line, (Figure 28c) represent changes in the life-style or a modification in occupational or career matters. Where there is an overlap, the new branch indicates the beginning of the new life or new job, generally a new direction in life. With overlapping lines it denotes a smooth transition from the old to the new life, usually initiated by the subjects themselves. A clean break, however, suggests a more sudden termination of the old life, more often than not instigated by others, as in the case of a redundancy, for instance (Figure 28d). The new life is taken up with renewed vigour when the next section of line appears.

It is the size of the gap or deviation in the line that marks the sort of difference from one phase of the life to the other. A slight kink here, as shown in Figure 28c, would suggest a small change such as a promotion or a side-step within the same company. A very wide space between the two sections of line (Figure 28e) implies a completely new start, a total change of career, a new environment and a different life-style altogether.

Islands in the line itself show periods of worry, possible disillusionment or frustration at work or at home or, in some instances, financial difficulties. Any bars seen cutting across the line reveal set-backs, interference or opposition to the normal course of events.

BRANCHES

Branches which rise towards the Fate line from the area of the Mount of Luna denote influences or relationships in the

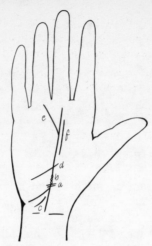

Figure 29. Markings on the Fate Line

subject's life. Should the branch actually meet and merge with the main line (Figure 29a) it denotes firm commitment or the consolidation of the relationship, usually marriage. Whether that relationship has a positive or negative effect on the individual can be judged by the appearance of the line immediately after the merger.

If the Fate line continues strong and straight then the relationship has a good effect. If, however, the line forms an island, or is interrupted by cuts or bars (Figure 29b), the relationship brings with it certain difficulties. If the Fate line breaks after the union and then starts again with a new section, the relationship creates changes, either signifying relocation or marking the beginning of a whole new way of life.

It has been shown that if an influence line from Luna fails to join into the Fate line, or if it cuts right through the main line, it bodes ill for that relationship (Figure 29c and d). Both these instances suggest that the relationship either won't last long at all, or it is likely to have a detrimental or disastrous effect on the subject.

Branches rising from the Fate line and reaching up towards the index mount are fairly uncommon but might show some form of public recognition. As that part of the hand represents anything connected with politics, the Church, the law and even education, a branch in this direction could imply success in any of those areas depending on the individual's career.

The normal ending of the Fate line is below the middle finger so it would seem most unlikely to find a branch rising up there.

Any branch rising towards the ring finger (Figure 29e) would highlight artistic or creative achievement, and possibly even success. Certainly, this branch indicates a feeling of satisfaction in the progress of the subject's career or way of life. Such a branch may actually double as an Apollo or Sun line.

A branch seen to rise towards the little finger implies some form of success connected with science, commerce, business or financial affairs, again depending on the individual's career.

PARALLEL LINES

If a branch is seen rising from the Luna mount and running parallel to the Fate line instead of meeting it, it is one of the best signs of an excellent partnership, usually indicating a good marriage where the two individuals feel more like partners than husband and wife.

Elsewhere along the course of the Fate line, a parallel line invariably indicates increased activity (Figure 29f).

ENDINGS

The normal ending for this line is on the mount of Saturn, below the middle finger, although it may terminate elsewhere on the hand.

If the line should suddenly stop on the Head line and does not resume at all, it is quite possible that a wrong move has seriously damaged the career. Ending suddenly on the Heart line might suggest that an emotional entanglement or setback (sometimes a major scandal) has had a detrimental, if not even a catastrophic, effect on the career. If the line swings over to end on the index mount it is possible that the subject could end up somehow in the public eye; even if not actually by becoming famous, at least by attaining some sort of public recognition or acclaim. If the ending sweeps over onto the Apollo mount beneath the ring finger, a career totally bound up with the Arts would be implied.

TIME ON OUR HANDS

Unlike astrology where the timing of events in our lives can be worked out with stunning accuracy if the exact details of birth are known, in hand reading the precise timing of events is not so satisfactory. Certainly, it is possible to establish the likelihood of particular events and occurrences on the hand within a certain time span, sometimes even down to an extremely narrow period of time, but it is still not possible to predict to the very month, let alone the actual day.

Nevertheless, the ability to assess whether something is likely to happen to us within the next few months as opposed to the next few years has its obvious merits, and it is preferable to not having any clues at all. The advantages of knowing the possible trends within our futures at least allows us time to plan our lives and to make contingencies within

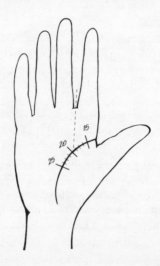

Figure 30. Time on the Life Line

that time. The beauty of timing events on the hand is that we can see for ourselves, in graphic detail, whether a line grows stronger or develops islands, bars, branches, changes direction or whatever.

There are various schools of thought as to the method of assessing and timing events. This is because hands do not come in uniform sizes, so any scale or gauge that is used has to be tailored for each individual. Accuracy does come fairly quickly after some practice, but it is wise, at the beginning, to establish a particular event, say an emotional upset or a house move which would be strongly marked and then to work out the rest of the timing from there. Even the experts do it this way. They like to confirm a couple of times and dates with their subjects first – especially so if the hand is smaller or larger than average – just to get their eye in, so to speak, and to enable them to modify their scale accordingly.

The Life, Head and Fate lines are used for this purpose. When it comes to timing, it is perhaps best to work from a print because then accurate measurements can be taken with a ruler.

TIME ON THE LIFE LINE

Time is read on this line from a starting point on the radial edge, below the index finger, around the thumb and down towards the wrist. Roughly one millimetre represents the span of a year, but care must be taken to compress or expand the scale according to the size of the hand. A good rule of thumb is to establish the twentieth year and work forwards and backwards from that point, and a quick method for setting this mark is illustrated in Figure 30.

Draw a line straight down from the inside edge of the index finger, and the point at which it meets the Life line marks roughly 20 years of age. From then on each millimetre can be marked off. After a while the measurements become so automatic that a ruler is not needed at all. Another good tip is to mark off 25, 30, 35, 40 and so on with a longer dash than the intermediate years, so that these can be picked out at a glance when analyzing the events on the line.

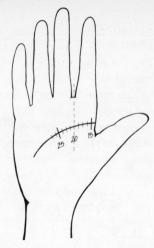

Figure 31. Time on the Head Line

TIME ON THE HEAD LINE

Timing events on this line is comparatively easy and is laid out in Figure 31. The 'millimetre-a-year' rule applies here and, as on the Life line, the twentieth year is established by drawing a line down from the inside edge of the index finger to touch the Head line. The age of 35 can also be established, this time by drawing a line from the centre of the middle finger down to meet the Head line. Yearly intervals can then be marked off using these two reference points.

TIME ON THE FATE LINE

The Fate line is read from the wrist up towards the fingers. Timing events on this line is not quite so straightforward as working on the Life line. The timing gauge for the Fate line is illustrated in Figure 32.

Measure the length of the palm from the top rascette to the base of the middle finger, and the halfway point represents 35 years of age. Now, 35 years are marked out evenly from the rascette up to this mid-way point but, from there on, the scale must be compressed lest we assume that every person's life span only reaches 70! Below 35, then, each year may be represented by a little more than a millimetre, above that point by a whole millimetre and then, possibly past the 50s, by even less. Remember that the scale must be modified further according to whether the hand is larger or smaller than would be normally expected.

As with the Life line, confirming the timing with a known event marking will help to adjust the gauge to suit.

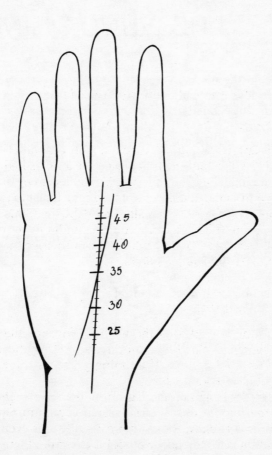

Figure 32. Time on the Fate Line

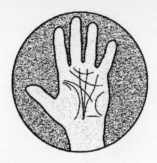

7 · THE MINOR LINES

Apart from the main creases in the palm, several other lines and markings may be found in the hand. Some people have many of these ancillary lines, giving their palms a 'busy' appearance (Figure 33). Others, however, have hardly any additional lines, resulting in a clear, uncluttered palm. The most well known of these minor lines and markings is probably the Sun line.

THE SUN LINE

The Sun line (Figure 33a) is also known as the line of Apollo. It may not be present in all hands, but when it is it shows:

- personal contentment
- satisfaction with the individual's life and work
- creative fulfilment
- success
- artistic talent and gifts
- luck with money
- fame

The Sun line works together with the Fate line for they seem to back each other up. Should one line show weaknesses, revealed by breaks or islands, the strength of the other would compensate for it. A good, strong Sun line denotes a person who is well-endowed with Apollonian characteristics,

98

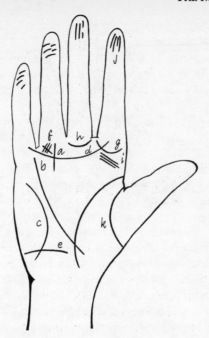

Figure 33. The Minor Lines

that is, outgoing, cheerful and creatively talented; someone who is warm and charismatic, and who possesses a sunny disposition.

BEGINNINGS

The line may rise from several points. If it starts from the base of the palm near the wrist (Figure 34a) it is a fairly rare sign of early success, such as a child actor or pop star might possess.

When the line springs from the Venus mount inside of the Life line, (Figure 34b), and shoots out to the Apollo mount, it denotes that the family has been responsible for contributing to the success of the individual. If the line rises like a branch from the Life line itself, and then makes its way to the Apollo mount (Figure 34c) success is attained through the individual's own achievements.

When the line develops from the Mount of Luna it is often a sign of public recognition and those who possess it often make their claim to fame either in the media or somehow in the public eye (Figure 34d). If the line commences a little higher up, on the Mount of Mars, success is achieved only via hard work (Figure 33a).

Springing from the Fate line and then rising upwards, as shown in Figure 29e, p.92, this Apollo line suggests an enhancement of the career itself, and adds to the individual's general feelings of contentment and satisfaction.

When it begins above the Heart line, this line suggests a comfortable old age coupled with a sense of well-being and peace of mind. It also implies that the subject will be surrounded by warmth and love in his or her latter years.

ABSENCE OF THE LINE

Sometimes the Sun line may not be present at all in a hand. Although this does not imply a complete lack of success, nor indeed abject failure, it does, nevertheless, show that life may

Figure 34. The Sun Line

not be quite as easy as it might and that success, if achieved, comes with struggle and hard work.

DOUBLING OF THE SUN LINE

People who have several Sun lines running side by side are the sort who tend to have many interests and, because of this, may not make a success of any at all. 'Jack/Jill of all trades and master/mistress of none' might be an appropriate epithet for them. If they like to have an active, buzzing life with masses of things to do, then many Sun lines would be appropriate; but this does suggest a scattering of energies over a large area rather than a concentration of effort on a single goal.

Traditionally, three Sun lines rising above the Heart line is a sign of luck when it comes to money and financial affairs. For these people, money seems to turn up, even at the last minute, just when they need it most. They may never become millionaires but at least they can be confident that they will never be totally without. Whether they have a knack in handling their money matters, or whether they are just born lucky, is a moot point; the plain fact of the matter is that when they need money, it appears like magic.

THE MERCURY LINE

This line is also known as the Health line, the Business line or the Hepatica (Figure 33b). It is a complex line to interpret mainly because insufficient satisfactory research has yet been carried out on it. It rises from anywhere around the base of the hand, frequently from the Venus or Life line area, and then rises to end on the Mercury mount under the little finger.

When present, the line represents aspects about the individual's:

- health
- business ability

The concept of *mens sana in corpore sano* is appropriate here since clear-headedness (due to a healthy constitution) leads to sharp and quick decision-making in any business dealings.

The presence of this line in the hand does not imply bad health, as has been thought in the past. It can, though, mean that these subjects are acutely aware of their nervous systems. It is interesting to note, however, that a poor Mercury line, that is islanded or frayed or twisted, can in fact denote a sensitive constitution and a lack of physical robustness.

It has also been thought in the past that the point at which the Mercury line cuts the Life line means certain death at that time. This is quite erroneous, and such nonsense simply spreads alarm. It is possible that such an indication may suggest ill health, or a weakening of the constitution at that point, but this must be judged according to its strength in comparison to the other lines and corroborated by health factors elsewhere.

THE BOW OF INTUITION

The Bow of Intuition (Figure 33c) appears as a semi-circular line on the percussion edge of the hand. People who possess this line are:

- highly intuitive
- perceptive
- incisive, with keen penetrating insight
- able to judge a situation or read someone like a book
- blessed with a sixth sense
- able to 'feel' what is going to happen in the future

The stronger and more complete the semicircle, the more sensitively perceptive the person is. Such people also have vivid, lucid and colourful dreams which, especially in times of trouble, may have more than a touch of precognition to them. If this formation is seen on the subjective hand alone, the owner has inherited this gift but has not developed it to its true potential. Those who have the line in a clear and strong formation on both hands should always rely on their instincts and be guided by their inner feelings.

THE GIRDLE OF VENUS

The Girdle of Venus (Figure 33d) is a semi-circular line which may be seen under the base of the fingers and above the Heart line. When present it denotes:

- creative talent
- extreme sensitivity

If the line is complete, extreme sensitivity may turn to suspicion or even paranoia. But if the line is broken or fragmented it shows that a good deal of common sense tempers that sensitivity, and the individual becomes receptive and sympathetic to others.

THE VIA LASCIVIA

When present, the Via Lascivia (Figure 33e) reveals:

- physiological sensitivities
- susceptibility to allergic reactions

People who possess this marking should take care with chemicals, alcohol, tobacco, drugs or other allergens, and with their diet in general. Because they may be allergic to any of these substances, they should also be aware that the presence of the line can also indicate a potential for addiction. Nowadays, the Via Lascivia is known as the allergy line.

THE MEDICAL STIGMATA

The Medical Stigmata is found on the Mercury mount below the little finger (Figure 33f). It consists of a series of three or more short vertical lines, with one crossing these horizontally. When present it denotes:

- natural healing ability
- empathy
- wonderful bed-side manner

Not everyone in the medical profession has this mark, nor indeed do all those who do possess it go into medicine. Many people who exhibit it have a soothing, compassionate nature, often emanating an aura of calm and serenity. Others use it actively, if not as doctors, nurses or vets, then in counselling roles or in helping those in need. Others find that they are able to 'soothe a furrowed brow', or bring active relief to those in pain, and particularly so to young children or animals, simply by running their hands over them. This is a special and wonderful gift and those who possess it should do all they can to develop it and use it therapeutically.

THE RING OF SOLOMON

The Ring of Solomon (Figure 33g) is a small semi-circular formation around the base of the index finger. When seen it shows:

- wisdom
- understanding
- balanced judgement

THE RING OF SATURN

This is another semi-circular formation which, when found, is seen around the base of the middle finger (Figure 33h). A fairly uncommon marking, it reveals:

- a negative attitude
- a time of frustration

This marking may come and go, fade or break up, and is usually seen during a period when the subject fights against a sense of frustration, a feeling that his or her footsteps are dogged no matter what he or she does. These people feel that they are forever being dragged back so that their endeavours amount to very little. If this attitude persists for a long time, owners of the ring of Saturn can end up rather bitter and extremely cynical about life.

SYMPATHY LINES

These are a series of oblique lines on the Mount of Jupiter below the index finger (Figure 33i). The formation highlights:

- great understanding of people and of life
- sympathy
- human warmth

LINES ON THE FINGER TIPS

Both horizontal and vertical lines may develop on the tips of the fingers from time to time (Figure 33j). Horizontal lines are a sign of stress and tension and usually come and go as pressures build up and are then resolved again. By simply establishing on which finger, or fingers, the greater concentration of lines occur, it is possible to gauge the source and nature of the problems affecting the individual.

Lots of horizontal lines on the index tip would suggest worry concerning the subject's ego or standing in life. Professional or occupational problems may be reflected here. On the middle finger, lines show anxieties regarding one's sense of security, property or home. On the ring finger, the lines hint at personal unhappiness, a sense of not being fulfilled and general dissatisfaction. Many horizontal lines on the little finger tip indicate worries concerning one's abilities of self-expression. Occasionally, lines here might also point to problems in the individual's sexual relationships.

Vertical lines on the finger tips are quite a different matter altogether. These areas of the hand are linked to the endocrine system, so it's possible that these markings may indicate hormonal imbalances depending on which of the finger tips are most affected. More research needs to be carried out in this area before any really conclusive evidence can be given.

At present it is believed that the index corresponds to the pituitary gland so vertical lines here might suggest faulty functioning of this gland. On the middle finger these markings throw suspicion on the mechanism of the pineal gland. On the ring finger there is a suggestion that vertical lines are linked with the thymus and are often found in the hands of people with faulty blood pressure (either high or low, depending on the subject's medical history). On the little finger vertical lines are connected with the thyroid gland. The conditions of hypo- or hyper-thyroidism may be marked in this way.

THE FAMILY RING

This is a curved line around the base of the thumb (Figure 33k). Any trauma line stemming from here, travelling across the Venus or Mars mounts and cutting the Life line, would indicate problems directly connected with one's parents, relatives or close family ties.

THE RASCETTES

The rascettes are the bracelets at the top of the wrist. Strong, well-formed rascettes are said to indicate a good constitution (Figure 35a). If the top rascette on the wrist bows upwards into the palm area (Figure 35b), it may indicate internal delicacy, and particularly gynaecological complications in women or urological problems in men.

ISLANDS, BARS, SQUARES AND STARS

Islands Whenever an island occurs in a line (Figure 36a), it tells of some form of weakening, or problems connected with the area represented by that line. On the Head line an island

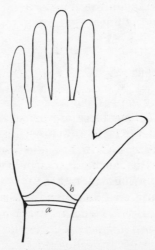

Figure 35. The Rascettes

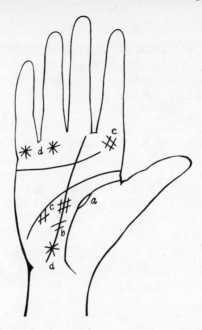

Figure 36. Islands, Bars, Squares and Stars

would suggest worry, whilst on the Life line it may indicate illness or a weakening of the constitution.

Bars A bar across a line (Figure 36b) is usually indicative of a temporary barrier, such as opposition, obstruction or some kind of interference in the normal course of events. The nature of the problem is often highlighted by other factors seen elsewhere on the hand and occurring at the same time.

Squares Squares (Figure 36c) are usually protective marks representing a buffer or cushioning effect to any unpleasant or injurious events illustrated on the hand. A square surrounding a break in the Life line, for instance, would suggest some form of protection against, perhaps, accident or danger.

The square is also an indicator of a period of hard work, when the individual will be called upon to exert a great deal of effort. In this case, the square formation will not sit *over* the line but will be found *attached* to it. This marking is more likely to be found attached to the Head or Fate lines.

Applying the timing gauge explained in Chapter 6 will give a fair idea of when the period of effort is likely to begin and end and thus how long the whole process will last.

Individuals with one of these formations in their hands will find that during this period of hard work they will probably feel plagued with frustration and a sense of limitation. They should treat that whole period as a valuable learning exercise. They need to keep their heads down, be constructive, concentrate their efforts and consolidate their knowledge. There will be times when they won't see the light at the end of the tunnel but they must trust that it *is* there and that they will see it in time. In this way they will be gradually laying down the foundations for their future.

If the square is attached to the Fate line, the effort is centred around the individual's career, occupation and responsibilities. If it's attached to the Head line, the work is more likely to be linked to the subject's mental, emotional or spiritual development.

One more square formation exists, which has a totally different interpretation to the other two. This is found on the Jupiter mount beneath the index finger and is known as the teacher's square. As its name implies, it reveals a natural ability to impart information to others. Not all those who possess this mark become teachers, and not all teachers have it in their hands, but those who do have a wonderful way about them, and especially with children.

Stars Tiny cross lines that form themselves into a star formation may occur either on a main line or may stand independently on any of the mounts on the palm (Figure 36d). The general rule is that a star on the line may represent a shock or an unexpected event, whereas independently on a mount it can denote success.

A star on the Head line, for instance, may show a time of mental crisis: a sudden major worry, or perhaps a physical injury to the cranium. On the Fate line it could indicate an unexpected or possibly alarming event. Instances of mental breakdown have been linked to stars on this line. On the Life line a star might suggest an accident.

The exception to this rule is a star on the Sun line. This does not bode ill in terms of a shock but denotes a surprise, the sort that brings some kind of luck or acclaim to the individual. Winning the pools, for example, might well be implied in this way. Becoming an over-night success, being awarded an MBE, having one's painting hung in the Royal College of Art or becoming a best-selling author may all be represented in this way as well.

A star standing proud on the mounts denotes success in whatever field is represented by that area of the hand and it must, therefore, be interpreted accordingly. However, a star on the Jupiter mount is exceptionally lucky as it augurs a successful life.

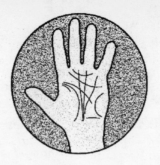

8 · RELATING

People's hands are brilliant reflectors of their emotions. Markings in the palms not only reveal how two people interact with one another but they can also give clues on their compatibility ratings and on what chances a couple has of successfully forming a happy relationship.

These clues lie in different areas of the hand and by working through the six levels outlined below, the information is built up, layer by layer, until a complete profile of the couple emerges.

LEVEL 1: COMPATIBILITY OF HAND SHAPES

The shape of the hand lays down the basic character of the individual, so those with similar shapes will have the same fundamental disposition. Bearing in mind that opposites can attract, there are various hand types which get on extremely well together because of their complementary nature, whilst others put together for any length of time would simply let the sparks fly!

Earth + Earth Two Earth types generally match each other well and would represent a solid, united, practical, sensible and hard-working couple of people. Stolidity, too little imagination and a lack of spontaneity might be on the negative side of this relationship.

Earth + Air Earth types are solid and love routine. Air types aren't and don't! But Air-handed folk are adaptable and inventive so they could find a happy compromise in this relationship. The practicality and common sense of the Earth partner could constructively help to both anchor and channel Air's imaginative ideas. Equally, Air could help to pep up his or her otherwise stolid partner. However, there is always the danger that Earth will frustrate Air, whilst Air's insatiable curiosity in life could drive the Earth partner to distraction.

Earth + Fire These two would certainly get on in terms of energy levels alone. They are both constantly on the go, active, busy beavers and, although the Fire partner might have more creative imagination, the Earth-handed counterpart would provide the practical application. On the negative side, Fire might over-stimulate and burn out the Earth partner, whilst Earth could put out Fire's enthusiasm for life in one fell swoop.

Earth + Water Perhaps the most disastrous combination of all. The stolid attitudes of the Earth partner would completely stultify the delicate sensitivities and ethereal qualities of the Water types. At the same time, Water's vagaries would jar at the logic and realism of the Earth-handed partner.

Air + Air Both compatible together, each would stimulate and excite the other.

Air + Fire Also compatible types; both have lively minds and buoyant dispositions.

Air + Water Air is emotionally too cool and distant for romantic Water, and Water too clingy for independent Air. But if they met on a creative and artistic plane there would be a fair chance of agreement here.

Fire + Fire Good compatibility. Both are restless and inventive so they would stimulate each other's imagination. Rivalry and competition, however, could spoil things between these two: both desire to be in the spotlight, both need adulation. If each can be understanding of the other's needs, this will work well. If not, neither is likely to waste any time in finding someone else who will.

Fire + Water This relationship has a lot to commend it.

Water + Water These two would certainly understand each other. They would be able to create a wonderful world of fantasy and fairy-tale around themselves, but there would be little grasp of reality. Would the shopping ever get done in this household, one wonders, and would the bills ever get paid?

LEVEL 2: COMPARISON OF FINGER LENGTHS AND SHAPE

The next step is to compare the fingers and thumbs for points of similarity or discord. The shape and length of the digits will reveal a person's attitude to his or her life and work.

Long fingers + long fingers Both would approach work in a careful, methodical way, patiently enjoying detail and minutiae. Perhaps there would be a little lack of spontaneity here though.

Short fingers + short fingers Both would share a quick, instinctive and intuitive way of dealing with life. Possibly the finger points and details in the everyday running of things would simply go by the board or would not even be noticed at all.

Long fingers + short fingers Excellent combination when able to work harmoniously together; potentially explosive otherwise. When they can work as a team the short-fingered person would be the wonderful organizer, splendid at making the plans and at setting up the projects. The long-fingered one can then take over to work out the refinements and fill in the details, whilst the short fingers can move on to the next project. When they don't see eye to eye it's because one is too fastidious whilst the other is too impulsive.

Lean fingers + fat fingers Lean-fingered folk tend to be more spiritually inclined than their fatter-fingered friends who are more earthy and materialistic. The lean fingers are able to tighten their belts philosophically when times are hard, whereas the fat fingers would suffer without their material security. Perhaps a little of lean's philosophy could help to ease life for the other during rougher times, and the fuller fingers could provide a touch of softness for their more ascetic friends.

Knuckled fingers + smooth fingers These two might annoy each other. The smooth-fingered people consider the long deliberations of the other as frustrating, and would often feel like shaking a response out of them. The knuckled-fingered partners, however, might wish their other halves would stop to think a little before apparently recklessly opening their mouths.

Weak thumbs + strong thumbs The stronger the thumb, the more strength of will and the more dominant the personality. The weaker the thumb the weaker the character. So, those with the stronger thumbs could use their forcefulness and dominance over the other, less determined types. Of course, it's quite possible that those with the weaker thumbs might prefer to be led and guided along by the others, especially if they also lack confidence in themselves.

Fingers widely spread + fingers tightly closed The wider the spread denotes a more open-minded and extroverted personality, whereas the other is more withdrawn, reserved and introverted. Problems here would result from the former being open, generous and socially gregarious whilst the latter is critical, suspicious and tenacious.

LEVEL 3: MATCHING FINGERPRINTS

Complementary or matching fingerprints will help the smooth running of the relationship as they reveal the fundamental nature of each partner and whether they will react to situations in similar ways.

Whorls + loops Whorls are the most fixed of all the pattern types and extremely slow to make up their minds. The loops, on the contrary, are quick, intuitive and need change for stimulation. Consequently, these two could really rub each other up the wrong way. In addition, owners of the whorl pattern need to be in charge and in control. It would only be the flexibility and pliant nature of the loops that would save the day here.

Whorls + arches A good combination. The arches are so good-natured that they could put up with anything, and the whorls could feel quite comfortable with the arched types knowing that their individualistic approach to life would not be challenged.

Whorls + composites These would get on because each takes time in the decision-making process. The fixity of the whorl could help the composite to become more decisive.

Loops + arches A wonderfully gentle and caring relationship.

Loops + composites Not at all bad together. Both are fairly mutable and each would be prepared to understand the other.

Arches + composites Again, an understanding and sympathetic pair.

LEVEL 4: COMPARING HEART LINES

Information gathered from comparing two people's Heart lines will reveal a great deal about their emotional compatibility. Illustrations of the different types of Heart lines may be seen in Figure 26, Chapter 6.

Rising up between the 1st and 2nd fingers This reveals warm and generous emotions, but these people find it difficult to express their feelings in words. They tend, instead, to make their emotions known through kind and loving deeds. Partners with this marking will need patient and gentle coaxing so that they can open up verbally and make known their innermost feelings.

Rising to the Mount of Jupiter These are the idealistic types who tend to be unrealistic about relationships. They see love and marriage through rose-tinted spectacles and relish dreams of romance, of knight errants and courtly love. They can be clinging types and because of their idealism they are emotionally vulnerable and get easily hurt. But if their romantic fantasies are indulged, these people will make loyal and loving partners. The higher the line climbs up the mount, the more jealous and possessive the person becomes.

Straight across towards the thumb edge Work comes first with these individuals and everything or everyone else must fit in around it. So be prepared to take second place if your partner possesses one of these!

Straight but ending under the middle finger Plenty of sex drive here, but not so hot when it comes to genuine affection and personal commitment. Be warned.

The Simian line Always a sign of emotional intensity. When it comes to relationships, those with the Simian line will be jealous and possessive. Forgiving and forgetting is definitely not a part of their make-up; partners with this formation will expect 100 per cent loyalty and faithfulness. Without that total commitment, this relationship will prove stormy and untenable.

LEVEL 5: COMPARING HEAD LINES

Does the couple share similar interests and attitudes? Do they have the same philosophy about life or the same point of view? The more they think alike or enjoy the same things together, the smoother their relationship is likely to be. A comparison of their Head lines will reveal intellectual compatibility. Illustrations of the different types of Head line may be seen in Figure 21, Chapter 6.

The straight Head line The straighter this line lies across the palm, the more logical and analytical the mentality. These people are born pragmatists; they are down-to-earth and fairly materialistic in their outlook. Business, commerce, finance, technology, science, mathematics and all practical matters are of interest. Partners with this line will bring a rational point of view into the relationship.

The curved Head line The more curved the line, the more creative, artistic, broad-minded and expansive the mentality. People possessing this type of line bring wider, outward-looking attitudes to the partnership.

The steeply curved Head line An exceedingly curved line, reaching right down to the Mount of Luna, suggests an over-active imagination, someone who is possibly moody and, in extreme cases, a person who could be manic-depressive. A practical, level-headed, no-nonsense type of partner would help this person to centre and balance his or her energies best.

The Simian line This denotes intensity. Such people are jealous and possessive. Putting up with their obsessions can place a strain on the relationship.

LEVEL 6: MATCH-MAKING

There are certain lines in the hand which give specific clues regarding marriage and love affairs. These are the Fate, influence and partnership lines. Illustrations to this level may be seen in Figure 29, Chapter 6. Branches which rise from the mount of Luna and then join the Fate line are recognized signs of relationships and are known as influence lines. It is the structure of these branches, together with the effect they have on the Fate line itself, which describes the nature and quality of the relationship in question.

If either the branch or the Fate line is broken or islanded after the merger, the relationship is rather troublesome and fraught with difficulties. Should the Fate line later strengthen, those difficulties would have been surmounted. When the branch actually merges with the main Fate line, the point of union is regarded as the time when the relationship actually consolidates itself, either in marriage or firm commitment of some kind. But if the branch doesn't actually touch or, indeed, if it crosses over the Fate line, this implies a rather disastrous or unhappy ending to the affair. Such a sign might exist, for example, if the intended partner doesn't turn up at the church on the wedding day. It is quite possible to time these events by reading off the scale on the Fate line as illustrated in Figure 32, Chapter 6.

The quality of the Fate line after the appearance of an influence line reveals the effects that the relationship has on the subject. If the main line continues strongly, the relationship has a positive effect; should the line become even stronger than before, the relationship would be immensely beneficial to the individual. Conversely, if the Fate line worsens, either by showing islands, fading or fraying, or if it is cut by crossing bars, it would imply that the relationship brings with it problems, complications and opposition. If, after the union of the influence line, the Fate line should break and a whole new section begins, it shows that the relationship has led to a completely new and different way of life for the people concerned (Figure 37a).

Sometimes a line rises from the Luna mount and, instead of joining the Fate line, runs along parallel to it (Figure 37b). This formation invariably indicates an excellent relationship and one which is based on the values of a partnership. Indeed, business partnerships are sometimes also marked out in this way.

Relationship lines can also occur inside the Life line and parallel to it (Figure 37c). The stronger the line the more important the relationship. The length of it does not necessarily indicate the duration of the relationship itself, but gives lots of clues regarding the influence it has on the subject.

It used to be said that marriage lines are seen lying horizontally on the percussion edge of the hand, just below the little finger. Investigation has disproved this theory as in many cases multiple lines exist on the hands of individuals who have only

Figure 37. Match-making Lines

enjoyed a single life-long marriage. However, an extension of one of these lines across the top of the palm and cutting the Heart line may represent that the subject will outlive his or her partner (Figure 37d).

Equally erroneous is the idea that vertical bars cutting through these so-called marriage lines represent children. Many such bars have been observed on the hands of people who have never had any children of their own but who have been somehow attached to youngsters in their lives: teachers, for instance, or favourite aunts and uncles. It is possible to detect the appearance of children in the hand as tiny branches which drop down from the inside of the Life line (Figure 37e). Once again, it is possible to date these events and influences according to the time scale on the Life line itself.

9 · HEALTH, WEALTH AND HAPPINESS

Recent medical research is confirming what the ancient palmists have known for centuries – that the hand can be a valuable aid in medical diagnosis. Hands can be used as maps which represent a picture of the physiological and genetic make-up of their owners, and so become rich potential indicators of health and well-being. These indicators can be detected in the hand at an early stage so that the subject can take preventive action, and, if possible, avoid the condition becoming a serious or chronic disorder.

There are three basic areas from which the trained eye can piece together the various clues relating to health:

- the temperature and colour of the skin and the nails
- the nature, construction and formation of the lines
- the pattern and condition of the fingerprints and skin ridges over the palm

Ideally, a healthy hand has an even temperature and colour, with a palm that is slightly lighter and pinker than the top. The nails are smooth and free from horizontal or vertical ridges, pittings or coloured specks. They should be pinkish in colour and springy along the length of the nail bed, with creamy-coloured moons. All the skin ridges are clear and sharp and the fingerprints are not obscured by cross lines on the tips. Both the major and minor lines are present, well-engraved and clearly defined. The fewer islands, chains, cross-bars or other adverse markings the better.

TEMPERATURE AND COLOUR OF THE HAND

The temperature of a hand should always be assessed according to the ambient temperature of the surroundings. For example, a hot hand on a hot day is quite normal, and should not necessarily be considered a clue to potential hyperthyroidism. Equally, any activity on the part of a subject prior to reading his or her hand should be noted. Hands dripping with perspiration after an aerobics class, for instance, don't automatically denote allergic sensitivities.

Bearing these factors in mind, observations of temperature and colour may denote the following:

- cold: poor circulation
- hot: feverish disposition
- dry, hot & rough: thyroid dysfunction (possible under activity)
- hot & moist: thyroid dysfunction (possible over-activity)
- hot & clammy: allergic reaction or toxicity
- cold & clammy: shock
- blue tinge: possible cardiovascular irregularities
- very white: anaemia
- yellow: jaundice, biliousness, liverish conditions

FINGERPRINTS

Recent medical research is beginning to throw important and exciting new light on fingerprints and patterns that make up the skin ridges. Studies have already confirmed that finger and palm prints are inherited. We also know that any developmental problems during the early weeks of foetal growth will imprint themselves into the skin markings of the hand. In this way, genetic or congenital malformations will be reflected in the actual fingerprints and in the ridge patterns that cover the palms.

Much research has already been carried out in this field, and a link has been firmly established between certain skin patterns and conditions such as Down's, Turner's and Klinefelter's Syndromes, all of which are a result of congenital defects and chromosomal abnormalities. Print 11, p. 72, is an example of a Down's Syndrome hand. Other conditions such as autism and childhood schizophrenia, for example, are also being examined in this light.

The studies seem to indicate that there are significant differences between the skin patterns of people with chromosomal disorders and patterns in normal hands. In general, fingerprints are less complex than in the normal hand, with perhaps more arches present, especially so with autistic children. In addition, skin ridges may be poorly formed or more broken up than usual. In the case of Mongolism, or Down's Syndrome, a higher proportion of patterns are found on the hypothenar, or Mount of Luna, and a significantly greater number of radial loops occur on the third and fourth finger tips. Radial loops sweep in from the thumb side of the hand, as opposed to ulna loops which sweep in from the percussion edge. (Figure 38).

It is possible that further studies in this area will enable physicians to use fingerprints and skin ridge patterning as an aid to genetic counselling.

At present, exciting new research is showing a connection between certain fingerprint patterns and heart disease. Researchers have found a correlation between a predominance of the whorl pattern and hypertension (high blood pressure), and heart disease, suggesting that people with a high proportion of whorls have a higher than average risk of developing cardiovascular diseases.

THE NAILS

The nails can be excellent indicators of health. On average, a nail takes about six months to grow from cuticle to quick, that is, to the top of the pink part of the nail bed. Nail production is

Figure 38. Loop Fingerprints

a continuous process, and any trauma – whether psychological or physiological – will cause a hiccough in the production, resulting in an instant fault marking in the nail.

Any ridging, pitting or spotting of the nail, which might imply a sudden illness, a shock or some form of dietary deficiency, can be used to date such an event. For example, if tiny dents exist about two-thirds of the way up the nails, it would suggest that the diet was poor and nutritionally out of balance about four months ago, perhaps caused by the individual going on a sudden crash diet.

Accidents or sudden shock may be represented by horizontal ridges on the nail. These are quite different to vertical ridges, which may result from allergic sensitivities and also from certain diseases such as rheumatic conditions. To confirm this, look for the Via Lascivia, or Allergy line, which often accompanies this type of ridging and thus corroborates the subject's sensitivity.

The colour and the construction of the nails can also give valuable clues to their owner's health.

• very white nails: possible sign of anaemia

- red nails: possible irregularities of the cardiovascular system
- blue nails: poor oxygenation, pulmonary or cardiac weaknesses
- poorly formed moons, either too large or too small: susceptibility to problems of the heart and/or lungs
- crooked or hooked nails: lung weaknesses/respiratory problems
- large cuticles: general mineral deficiencies
- white spots: zinc imbalance (aggravated by emotional problems)
- pits, dents, dished or convex nails: dietary problems, imbalance of minerals and vitamins

THE LINES

For best effect, lines should be well engraved and solid in construction; any breaks suggest either physiological or psychological changes. Islands split the energies represented by the particular line on which they are found, and thus suggest a weakening of the function during the time they are present. This may be manifested as a weakening of physical strength, if seen on the Life line, or a time of worry, anxiety and problems in general if found on the other main lines. Chaining suggests mineral deficiencies or chemical imbalances and should be further investigated in order to correct the condition implied.

SPECIFIC AILMENTS

Allergies

Individual sensitivity to particular foodstuffs, chemicals, drugs, and so on is a most interesting study, and one which is receiving increasingly sympathetic treatment. Although the hand doesn't give any magic formulae for detecting which allergens an individual is especially sensitive to, it can offer a means for detecting those people who are *more likely* to be susceptible to allergies.

Two areas in the hand highlight allergic sensitivity. The first is seen in nails which have heavy vertical ridges. The second is seen by the presence of the Via Lascivia, or Allergy line. This lies across the bottom third of the palm, entering from the percussion edge and cutting across the Luna mount on its way towards the Life line.

Eyes, Teeth and Ears

Any problems connected with the eyes, teeth or hearing may be detected on or above the Heart line. An island in this line immediately under the ring finger (Figure 39a) often suggests problems with sight, and anyone possessing such a formation should have their eyes checked regularly.

A patch of fine hair lines situated below the ring and little fingers and lying just above the Heart line often signifies dental problems (Figure 39b).

An island in the line below the index or middle fingers may denote hearing problems (Figure 39c). Detecting this marking in the hands of a youngster can be extremely valuable since such defects can often be remedied if early medical attention is sought.

Headaches

Headaches, dizziness, sinus problems and general difficulty in concentration are all reflected in the Head line. Migraine, for example, is represented by tiny indentations in the line (Figure 39d). These look like pin-pricks; if the headaches come in regular bouts, these tend to occur in clusters along the line, but if the migraine attacks are sporadic the indentations stand separately. When a concentration of these can be detected in the future some sort of preventive action may be possible.

If the line itself broadens out at any point and becomes rather fuzzy, it represents a period when clarity of thought is lacking, when there is a marked loss of concentration and possibly some dizziness too (Figure 39e). These conditions could be

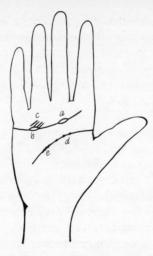

Figure 39. Signs of Health on the Hand

due to anxieties and worry, perhaps from work pressures or emotional upheavals, or from some clinical reason such as sinusitis. Any underlying psychological problem may be confirmed by a trauma line cutting either the Life, Fate or Head lines. If it's physiological in nature, an island somewhere on the main lines may pinpoint the source.

Cardiovascular Problems

Cold, blue hands, or a bluish tinge around the base of the nails, are clues to possible circulatory, heart or lung problems. A bright red hue to the nails can indicate an irascible temperament which traditionally became associated with apoplexy or strokes.

The Heart line is the obvious area to analyze when looking into cardiovascular problems, although not enough scientific evidence exists to confirm any specific conditions. However, it is believed that a break in the line, a deep, red indentation or a star formation on the line may denote a susceptibility to cardiac disease and heart attacks (Figures 40a, b, c). It has also been suggested that tiny pin-pricks around an island in this line may indicate the possibility of angina pectoris (Figure 40d).

Digestive Disorders

Those who suffer from dyspepsia, intestinal acidity, nervous or 'gippy tummy', or any problem of the digestive or alimentary tract, may possess a patch of whispy, sometimes twisted, lines that rise obliquely upwards, clustering around the Health line between the Life and Heart lines (Figure 40e). The Health line may also be twisted and ragged. This marking advises that the diet needs to be reassessed.

Poor nutrition may also be corroborated by nails which are dished or pitted. Severe crash diets are often registered by a horizontal groove on each nail.

Hormonal or Endocrinal Conditions

It has been observed that a connection exists between the glands of the endocrine system and vertical lines etched into the tips of the fingers. Although a great deal more study needs to be carried out, it is believed that imbalances of the pituitary, the pineal, the thymus and the thyroid glands are linked in turn with the index, second, ring and little finger tips.

Vertical lines on the tip of the little finger have certainly been observed on people with either an over or under active thyroid gland, or who at least have a history of thyroid conditions in their families. There is growing suspicion that as well as linking with the thymus, such lines on the tip of the ring finger may allude to irregularities in blood pressure. Whether then, by implication, the thymus gland has any responsibility for regulating the blood flow through the system is open to debate.

Little concrete evidence exists that firmly establishes a link between the other two glands and the first and second fingers. However, it has been observed that when an individual's

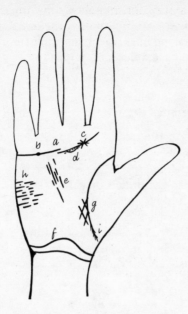

Figure 40. Signs of Health Problems on the Hand

hormones are behaving erratically, as may happen during the menopause, *all* the finger tips become vertically lined, suggesting that the general health or the body chemistry of the individual is out of balance.

Mineral Deficiencies

Mineral imbalances show up on the nails either in the form of white specks (which could suggest a calcium and/or zinc deficiency) or by the fact that the nails are brittle, split easily, grow discoloured or distorted.

Heavily islanded Heart lines or strongly chained Head lines also point to vitamin/mineral imbalances, and in these cases the diet ought to be investigated.

Iron deficiency anaemia may be detected instantly when the palm is stretched and the main lines appear white or washed out instead of running a healthy pink or beige colour (depending on race). Sometimes lines on women's hands may lose their colour temporarily after menstruation when there has been heavy blood loss and consequently a loss of iron. Eating leafy green vegetables, or taking a suitable tonic, would soon right the condition.

Respiratory Disorders

Susceptibilities to pulmonary problems such as bronchitis, pneumonia, even heavy colds and chesty coughs are represented by islands at the top of the Life line, and especially so if these occurred as childhood diseases. Islands in the Health line would also confirm this tendency.

Few, or even non-existent, moons, or nails that curve around the finger tips, are also signs of possible lung weaknesses and poor oxygenation. The markedly curved nail is a particular feature sometimes seen on the hands of heavy smokers.

Problems of the Reproductive System

Problems relating to both the male and female reproductive organs are reflected in two areas located at the base of the palm. The first is in a distorted top rascette which markedly arcs from the wrist up onto the palm (Figure 40f). This invariably denotes internal weaknesses of the reproductive system.

The second indication of a predisposition to complications here can be seen in a triangular or diamond-shaped formation of lines which lies about one-third of the way up from the wrist and which is attached to the outside of the Life line, (Figure 40g). In a man's hand it can warn of potential uro-genital problems, although it has also been found in men with a predisposition to hernia. In a woman's hand it may reflect gynaecological complications which can range from simple irregularities of the menstrual cycle right up to the need for a hysterectomy.

If this sign is detected, preventive action may be taken, or regular medical checks could pick up any irregularities early enough to treat the condition before it ever became a serious problem.

Rheumatic Ailments

Advanced stages of rheumatism and arthritis can be seen by the inflammation and/or distortion of the joints and knuckles.

Clues to a build-up of uric acid, believed to be implicated in certain gouty or rheumatic conditions, may be detected on the percussion side of the palm in the form of tiny hair lines lying obliquely in a patch over the Mounts of Mars and Luna (Figure 40h). Close examination of these fine lines reveal that they are caused by a breaking down of the skin ridges and it is the extent of this veiling, as it is called, that reveals the degree of acidity in the system. Those possessing any such veiling should check their diets and modify their intake of highly acidic foods.

Senility and Problems of Old Age

The last section of the Life line deals with the retirement age of the individual, and any obstruction or impairment of the line here would reflect either physical or psychological problems at this time of life. Fine lines dropping down from this area denote general debility, a lack of robustness and a draining or dissipation of energy (Figure 40i).

Such problems as senility or memory loss may be detected on the Head line. Any island present on the last section of the line would show mental weakness and forgetfulness, whilst fraying, breaking or thinning out at the end is often a sign of impending senility. When these indicators are seen it might be advisable to set up projects or embark on a course of treatment or mental exercises which would help to strengthen the mind and thus avoid the effects that such mental weakening would imply.

Stress

Signs of stress and tension may be registered in many ways on the hand, but two unmistakable indicators may be picked up easily: horizontal lines across the finger tips, and a palm that is covered in a cobweb of lines.

Tiny horizontal lines forming across the finger tips are prime indicators of stress. The crux of the problem is denoted by the greater concentration of these lines on particular fingers.

- *On the index* Problems concerning the subject's ego and standing in the world. Perhaps pressure stems from the work place or from the person's career.
- *On the middle finger* Problems centre around the home and the subject's sense of security. Stress over property matters may be reflected here.
- *On the ring finger* Personal unhappiness, discontentment and disillusionment are marked here. Relationship problems are often reflected by lines across this finger tip.
- *On the little finger* Problems over one's self-expression and sometimes also with sexual relationships and communications are presented here.
- *On the thumb* A cluster of cross lines across this tip suggests that problems in general are having an adverse effect on the individual's nervous system.

Getting to the root of the stress and tension is easy when the markings appear only on one finger tip. More often than not, though, because our problems spill over into all the other areas of our lives, it's more usual to find that several, if not all, the digits become affected to some degree. In that case, it's the finger with the greatest number of these lines which holds the key.

Sometimes a combination of finger tips might be involved. For instance, markings on both the middle and ring fingers, could suggest that happiness and home life (that is, the sense of security) are on shaky territory because of family, marital or financial problems. Once the areas of concern have been identified in this way, an analysis of the rest of the hand should give further clues and confirm the problem.

The second indicator shows at a glance whether an individual is a natural worrier and thus prone to stress and tension. This is seen in a palm that is literally covered in lines and which looks as if a spider has woven its web all over it. A palm like this is known as a 'full hand' (Print 13).

The opposite of the 'full hand' is called an 'empty hand'.

130

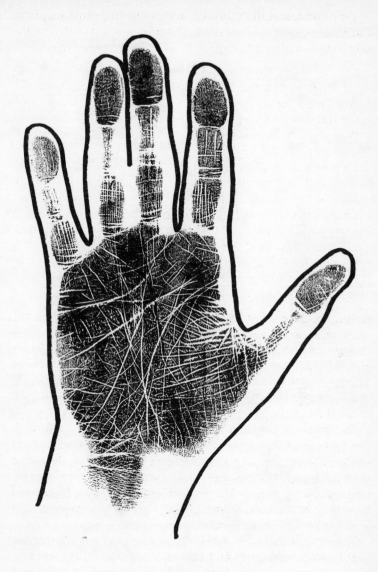

Print 13. The 'Full' Hand

A comparison of the two highlights how apt their titles are: the former crammed to the gunwales with lines, and the latter containing the bare essential three or four.

The more lines in a hand, the more sensitive the individual, so people with full hands tend to be more highly strung and more disposed to nervous worry. In contrast, those with an empty hand are rarely ill, for it's as if they're unaware that they possess a nervous system at all! These people are more likely to shrug off the everyday anxieties which the fuller-handed folk might allow to build up into stressful situations which then become potentially adverse to health.

WEALTH

Markings that throw the spotlight on finances, whether inheritances, legacies, lucky wins or simply money that's accumulated through the individual's own efforts, can be seen in various ways throughout the hand.

Scooping the jackpot or winning the pools may be rare, but if it should happen it could well be registered by a line from the Venus mount rising up to the ring finger and ending in a star (Figure 41a). Financial backing from the family is shown by a line from the Venus mount, or else one peeling out from the Life line, and shooting its way up towards the middle finger (Figure 41b). Inheritances, some say, appear as curved lines swinging in from the percussion side of the palm and sweeping up to the Apollo mount beneath the ring finger (Figure 41c).

A set of three lines above the Heart line traditionally suggests that its owner is lucky with money. It doesn't necessarily mean that people with this formation will become millionaires, but that whenever they need money it just seems to appear in the nick of time. Whether it is that they are born lucky or simply that they have a knack with money is unclear. Certainly the message is that these people shouldn't worry unduly about money; when they need it something invariably turns up.

Branches from the Head line that sweep up towards the little finger often suggest intellectual or career successes such as promotions, for example, which are often accompanied by

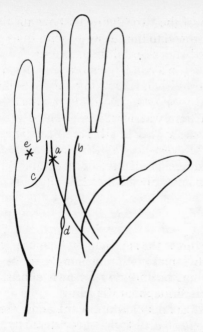

Figure 41. *Signs of Wealth on the Hand*

salary increases. For those running their own businesses, this marking might denote expansion, successful business deals or buying and selling at a profit. Islands in these branches, or more often in the Fate line, point to financial problems and restrictions (Figure 41d). An island on the Fate line in particular warns of a time when belts need to be tightened. Should the island be spotted in advance, the subject is advised to check nest-eggs or insurance policies carefully in order to avert any future problems.

Traditionally, a ring finger that is longer than the middle one is a sign of the gambler. Whether the individual will be successful or otherwise will be revealed by other financial indicators elsewhere in the hand.

A star on the Mercury mount promises success in business and thus by implication financial success too (Figure 41e). A star on the Mount of Apollo augurs fame and recognition which is invariably accompanied by monetary gains and rewards. But a star on the Jupiter mount, beneath the index finger, is the clearest indication of a successful and financially buoyant life.

HAPPINESS

The Sun, or Apollo, line is perhaps the best indicator of a sense of happiness. This line lies vertically in the hand and sweeps up in the direction of the ring finger. Although it is generally considered a sign of success it does, in actual fact, represent a sense of satisfaction and fulfilment in its owner.

If, for instance, motherhood should bring that sense of fulfilment and achievement, then the Sun line would develop on that hand at the time the feeling was realized. On a different hand, the line might be read as indicating peace of mind after a long period of emotional problems. Yet again, it is possible that the Sun line could stand for public acclaim. The line has several interpretations according to the individual, but in general it highlights improvement and a better sense of well-being in the quality of the subject's life.

The Sun line may begin at any point in the hand, but it must push its way up to (or at least towards) the Apollo mount. If the line is long and strong, commencing down near the wrist, the individual is likely to achieve success and, presumably, happiness from a very early age. Although this feature is rare, it does exist in the hands of those who might be called 'child stars', revealing the sunny and charismatic personality and disposition that would propel that person into prominence at such an early age.

A line beginning on the Luna mount and sweeping up to Apollo shows public favour and recognition. An actor, a favoured politician or anyone in the public eye might have this marking (Figure 42a). Beginning higher up, above the Heart line, this formation suggests that the sense of true happiness and contentment begins much later on in life, often in retirement, but it is a splendid augury for an old age filled with warmth, love and understanding.

Several parallel Sun lines may denote a person who has many diverse interests and who takes great pleasure in all of them. It might be said that these people may never become successful in anything in particular as they divide their attention instead of concentrating on one major objective. If, however, this is their way of deriving satisfaction and fulfilment then surely this is right for them.

Obviously the stronger the line the better the expression of success and happiness. But should the line be broken or fragmented it would show that these feelings are rather spasmodic. Traditional palmistry states that an island seen in the Sun line reveals a scandal, and in some cases this might be true (Figure 42b). The suggestion of notoriety or of getting a bad press through this time, for example, could be represented in this way in the hand.

Generally, though, such a formation would suggest a period of frustration and dissatisfaction, when plans may be thwarted and ambitions put on hold. The composition of the line after this event tells how the individual overcomes the difficulties implied. If the line strengthens again, the reputation or peace of mind is restored. But if the line breaks up and peters out, it would suggest that the difficulties are not reconciled and the individual is left feeling that his or her reputation has been irrevocably damaged.

Comparing and contrasting this line with other markings in the hand confirms both the reason for its growth and the events represented by it. For example, if the line should begin to grow at the same time that a large island on the Head line comes to an end, it can be assumed that the individual has come through a period of worry and indecision and has found direction and satisfaction.

Should the growth of the line coincide with a marriage, a move or a birth in the family, it would be these events that register upon this line as bringing deep contentment to its owner. If coincidentally a new section of Fate line is seen, or a rising branch off the Head line, the growth of the Sun line at the same time will confirm that changes taking place within the subject's career will be for the better.

Likewise, adverse events can be checked off on this line. For instance, if an island exists in the Sun line it could coincide with a broken influence line, thus revealing that a troublesome

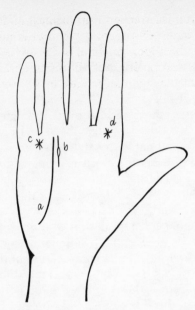

Figure 42. Signs of Happiness on the Hand

relationship is responsible for the individual's unhappiness. If a break in the Sun line is seen at the same time as an island in the Life line, it could be that an illness is marring the individual's sense of contentment.

It is important, then, to examine the point of origin of this line, as well as its construction and composition, and to link the information to the rest of the indications seen. In this way it is possible to construct a clear picture of the progress of the individual's success and ideas of happiness in his or her life.

One final important marking connected with happiness and success is the star, which is formed by a cluster of little lines all crossing a particular spot. They may occur across a main line or be found standing independently on a mount. There are two locations in the hand where the occurrence of a star is especially significant in this respect.

The first location is on the Apollo mount beneath the ring finger (Figure 42c). A star here suggests the sort of accomplishment that could take the individual into the public eye. It usually promises recognition for past endeavours and sometimes even fame. The second location is on the Mount of Jupiter under the index finger (Figure 42d). Here, a star is perhaps in the best position of all as it highlights a strong potential to succeed in whatever area of life the individual may choose.

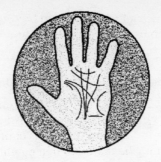

10 · CAREER GUIDANCE

More and more people are beginning to recognize the value of handreading when it comes to advice about careers and occupations. A good analysis can help to:

- steer youngsters in the right direction
- detect hidden talents
- encourage late developers
- make the right career choices
- advise on mid-career dilemmas
- give advance warning of impending problems or opportunities
- sort out personality clashes between work colleagues
- highlight pitfalls or openings when setting up in business

What's more, guidance and occupational advice can be given throughout an individual's career. Major decisions regarding changes of jobs or professions, crises at work, power struggles, problems with colleagues or superiors, the question of retirement and many, many more issues connected with the individual's working life can be clarified in this way. Examining future trends in the hands can also provide advance warning of the possibility of such occurrences well in advance.

Matching individuals to suitable types of jobs, analyzing job prospects, teasing out markings that reveal latent talents and then extracting information on the general progress of a person's working life may be achieved by running through the following four steps.

STEP 1: HAND SHAPE

Because of the character and personality it represents, each basic hand shape is more suited to certain types of jobs than to others. When applying the fundamental principles, however, it must be borne in mind that not all hands conform neatly to the pure types; some may be made up of a combination of several different types. This means that the owner of a combination hand may fit into a broader spectrum than at first appears. Additionally, each of the four steps modifies the whole so that the complete pattern of the working life doesn't emerge until each piece of information has been collected and laid one on top of the other. Shapes of hands can be checked in Chapter 2.

EARTH HANDS

Key Aspects Earth-handed people are perhaps the hardest workers. They are practical and down-to-earth, preferring to plod along in a routine way. Anything that takes them out of doors is preferable to being cooped up in a stuffy office all day long. Because of their earthy nature, these people make very contented farmers or gardeners, and enjoy anything that takes them close to the soil. Indeed, anything which enables them to work with their hands gives these people immense satisfaction.

On a different level, the logical pragmatism that some of them display could happily take them into banking or accountancy. For others who incline more towards discipline, law and order, anything connected with the police force, or the armed forces, would suit. Since they like to work in a rather systematized way, they would be able to cope with any routine or repetitive job, such as assembly or production line work.

AIR HANDS

Key Aspects Air-handed folk tend to be creative and need a lot of variety. They are intellectually lively types who can be stimulated by all kinds of challenges. They are at their best working with other people in an open, flexible atmosphere where the free exchange of news and views buzzes around. They are extremely quick learners, and make good businessmen and women because they have a knack for organization and are able to make snappy, instinctive judgements and decisions. They are equally happy in the financial, secretarial and commercial worlds. Because of their passion for communications anything to do with information technology, literary work, the travel industry or computer technology would suit them down to the ground. They make fine speakers and many are excellent linguists.

Putting together their flexibility, creativity and love of new ideas with their need to work in a buzzy atmosphere, Air-handed folk are made for the media and many gravitate towards journalism, publishing and occupations in the film industry, in broadcasting and in television.

FIRE HANDS

Key Aspects Physically and mentally active, people with Fire-shaped hands always seem to have a lot of pent-up energy. They like to keep busy and have a tendency to launch themselves enthusiastically into whatever project currently takes their imagination. Born extroverts, they are essentially crowd-pullers and happiest in the lime-light, which is why many find themselves in the world of entertainment. The more theatrical or flamboyant the occupation, the more it suits them. Taking charge comes naturally so they make excellent managers and organizers. Their abilities to shoulder responsibility, to make decisions on the spur of the moment together with their brilliant skills in man-management and in coping with stressful situations make them natural leaders in whichever field they choose. As politicians, lecturers, members of the clergy or officers in the forces, they reveal a talent for inspiring and motivating others. Indeed, wherever they are, these people seem to be able to rally the troops with their infectious zest for life. With their inspirational creativity they make good designers, artists and sculptors; with their intrepid daring, they enjoy explorations, pioneering work, being at the cutting edge. And their need to help others can bring many into consultancy work or into the various caring professions.

WATER HANDS

Key Aspects The long, lean Water hand belongs to those who tend to be unpredictable and impractical when it comes to worldly affairs. They are the dreamers who have a strong appreciation of beauty and aesthetics. The Water hand highlights the spiritual and belongs to the poets and fine artists of the world; and if they don't actually practise the arts themselves, they certainly have a tremendous appreciation for them. Novelists, too, who live in the realms of fiction and fantasy, would more often than not possess this hand type and the literary world would be lost without them. Because they are perceptive, they can also make excellent psychoanalysts. Equally, their sensitivity regarding human nature can turn them into very fine actors and musicians, whilst their sense of culture and refinement could take them into the beauty trade or anything connected with the glamour industry.

STEP 2: THE HEAD LINE

Because the Head line is the indicator of intellectual abilities, it reveals not only *how* individuals think but also *what* they think about. In career guidance, a mere glance at this line reveals the general area the subject is suited to, whether the inclination is more towards the Arts or to the Sciences.

The straighter the line, the more practical, down-to-earth and logical the mentality. This is the sort of mind that applies itself to the more rational, materialistic and concrete subjects. Anything connected with business, science, commerce or technology would suit the owners of this sort of line. Matters based on fact interest these people most; anything of an airy-fairy nature will turn them off. Thus it may be said that people with straight Head lines tend to be convergent thinkers.

The shorter and higher up the line, the more the mind is focused on mundane and materialistic affairs. The interests and conversations of their owners tend to revolve around material possessions and security – cars, money, property, holidays – anything that has tangible worth and that can be considered *real*, as opposed to abstract concepts.

The curved line denotes the artistic, creative and imaginative mind. These people are more inclined towards the arts, music, literature, languages and communications in general. Mentally, they are much more expansive and divergent in their thinking than those with the straighter lines. The deeper the curve, the more extreme becomes the imagination. Owners of Head lines that reach right down into the Mount of Luna should find an outlet for their rich, artistic talents in the world of fine arts, in design or fiction writing. Without a focus, such a strong imagination can all too easily tip itself into melancholy or develop into bouts of moodiness and depression.

Half straight and half curved combines both the pragmatic and creative ways of thinking (Figure 43a). People with this line can be found in the occupations suitable to either type. They may find it extremely hard at first to choose which way to go and, sometimes, they may reach a crisis half-way through their careers and change course altogether. The trick is to find a happy compromise; an occupation or a line of work that combines structure with creativity and allows the interplay of practicality with imagination.

A writer's fork, that is, a line that forks beneath the ring finger, suggests heightened powers of creativity. Anyone with this formation would do well to pursue a career in the Arts, in the media, literary or publishing worlds.

People with Simian lines do best in occupations where they need to focus their attention or use deep concentration. For example, sportsmen and women, who need to be single-minded in order to succeed, are helped enormously by the characteristics denoted by this line. Alternatively, anything requiring deep investigation would also suit.

In terms of length, it is usually considered that the shorter the line, the more materialistic the mentality, whereas the longer it is, the more scope there is for intellectual thought. Although not always the case, this theory holds good as a general rule. However, the quality of the line, as well as its

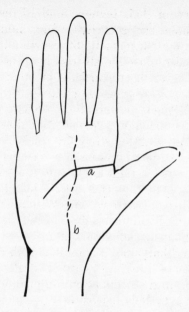

Figure 43. Career Progress on the Head and Fate Line

length, must also be taken into consideration. Breaks, islands, chains or feathering all weaken the intellectual potential. Such negative markings reveal worries and problems that lead to a lack of concentration and difficulty in decision-making. But a clear, unbroken line highlights clarity of thought and a lively, vibrant mentality.

STEP 3: THE FATE LINE

Whilst the shape of the hand and the type of Head line suggest the sort of occupation an individual is suited to, the Fate line actually charts the events that are likely to take place and changes which may occur within that person's career. In addition, by measuring the Fate line, it is possible to date precisely when those events are likely to occur.

A break anywhere along the line denotes a change within the individual's career. If the line ends and a new section overlaps the old, the change of job will occur through the individual's own instigation. If a tiny deviation in the course of the line is seen, or if the gap between the two overlapping ends is very slight, the likely impact would be small, or perhaps there would simply be a change of emphasis, such as a promotion or a side-step within the same company. The wider the gap between the two overlapping ends, the bigger the change. This could suggest taking up a new occupation, possibly involving a move to another part of the country.

If, however, the line comes to an abrupt halt and doesn't resume until higher up, it is an indication that changes within the occupation have been made outside the individual's control. This can often be one of the signs of redundancy, and is of obvious value if it is picked up well in advance because contingency plans can be worked out and put into effect. The resumption of the line shows when the normal working life is taken up again.

When a section of the line is wavy, fragmented or very faint it can indicate a period of vacillation, when the individual is in and out of work or tries out one job after another (figure 43b). When the line consolidates and strengthens, it can be said that the individual has found direction and purpose not only in occupational matters but also in life in general.

Any tiny bars cutting through the line signify obstruction or opposition. This might be seen if there is any industrial strife, problems with workmates, personality clashes or disagreements with colleagues or bosses. Islands in the line, however, invariably indicate financial difficulties.

An analysis of the line after the event marking will reveal the outcome. For example, if the line should strengthen considerably after a break, it shows that the change has been a positive one. But if the line is weaker, or becomes chained or fragmented, it can be seen that the change has brought added difficulties or complications to the subject.

STEP 4: SPECIAL MARKINGS

Individual markings with special relevance to occupational matters are found all over the hand. Possessing any one of these markings doesn't automatically mean that an individual is predestined to a particular job. What it does mean, though, is that the person possesses natural talents and skills which make him or her more suited to a certain type of career.

THE HEALING HAND

Invariably found on the hands of people in the caring profession or in the medical fields, the medical stigmata (Figure 44a) is composed of several tiny oblique lines, more often than not with a horizontal bar cutting across them, situated above the Heart line and beneath the web between the third and fourth fingers.

The medical stigmata is a special marking which denotes a natural gift for healing. Whether the gift is used in orthodox or complementary practice, in clinical or counselling situations, makes no difference. Whenever it is seen, it always implies a kind, caring, therapeutic nature, someone who is a good listener and who can help to ease the pain.

THE FARMER OR GARDENER

The Earth hand is most associated with farmers and horticulturists. Often a long basal phalanx on the middle finger is a good sign of someone who is a keen gardener and who is lucky enough to possess green fingers (Figure 44b). If seen on the Water hand, this feature may indicate the landscape gardener.

One especially rare marking is a skin loop lying across the Mount of Luna and entering the palm from the percussion edge (Figure 44c). This feature denotes a rare sensitivity to, and understanding of, flora and fauna, so those who possess this marking have an inherent rapport with Nature.

THE CRAFT WORKER

People who work with their hands may have any of the basic hand shapes, but the one feature they all share is the pronounced angular base to the thumb known as the angle of

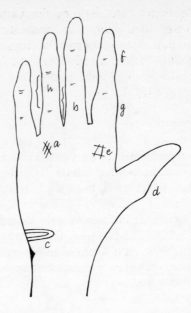

Figure 44. *Special Markings Relating to Career*

manual dexterity (Figure 44d). In addition, those with very long fingers will be especially methodical and painstaking with detail and consequently don't like to be rushed over their work. Their shorter-fingered colleagues, though, pick up new skills at a glance and work fast, taking a broader view and a more inspirational approach to the job.

TEACHERS AND ACADEMICS

Though drawn from all the hand categories, good teachers and lecturers may well find they possess the teacher's square, a small box-like formation found on the mount beneath the ring finger (Figure 44e). This invariably reveals a natural gift for imparting information to others.

Long top phalanges denote an intellectual approach to life, and when the top phalanx of the middle finger is particularly long it tells of a love of research. A noticeably tapered basal phalanx on this finger also denotes the perpetual student, someone who takes great delight in constantly learning new things. In addition, if all the joints of the fingers are markedly pronounced, other than through illness or injury, this becomes known as the philosophical hand, and represents the hand of the thinker (Figure 44f).

THE SPORTY HAND

People who are involved in active or contact sports invariably have strong, muscular-looking hands. The seat of energy, or the power-house, is located at the base of the palm, so that if the owner's Mounts of Venus and Luna are well-developed the individual has plenty of vitality and physical stamina, and this characterizes the active sportsman. Women who play sports, though, may not have such a prominently muscular base to their plams but may possess more wiry hands which would signify fitness and robustness.

THE CREATIVE HAND

One of the instantly recognizable signs of this hand is the bowed percussion edge. A curved Head line, too, reveals an imaginative, expansive and divergent mentality. If the fingers are short on the creative hand there will be instinctive and inspirational flair. But if the fingers are long, patience and attention to detail will be the motivating force. The angle of manual dexterity will also highlight those who enjoy working with their hands.

THE SOLDIER'S HAND

The Earth or Fire hands would be the most suitable shapes for those suited to the armed forces. Both have the basic toughness that is required in this field. Characteristically, the Mount of Lower Mars should be large or well-developed as this suggests both courage and a certain aggressive strength. Such leaders of men can also have extra-long indices, although this in itself can be a sign of the tyrant or dictator. It has been said that both Napoleon and Hitler had longer index fingers than their middle ones.

THE HAND OF THE OFFICE WORKER

With offices becoming increasingly mechanized, computerized and ultra hi-tech, the Air hand would be quite at home in this environment. Communications are the first love of those with this hand type, and messing about with state-of-the-art gadgets is their second.

Both straight and curved Head lines would fit in with office life, given that the nature of the work is congenial to each of them. The former denotes a practical and logical approach to the work, whilst the latter brings imaginative talents and a flair for dealing with the general public.

THE CATERER'S HAND

The hands of cooks and caterers are typified by full, well-developed basal phalanges on all the fingers, but especially so on the index (Figure 44g). If this phalanx is somewhat longer and, although full, is firm, it would suggest the gourmet. Very often, restaurateurs have this feature prominently marked in their hands. The good housekeeper and, equally, the person who has a gift for management and husbandry, is marked out by long middle phalanges on all the fingers (Figure 44h). This is also the classical sign of efficiency.

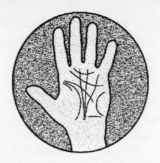

11 · COPING WITH THE UNFORESEEN

There is no doubt that one of the most positive advantages of hand analysis is that it provides a glimpse into possible future events and occurrences. Although it must be stressed that such indications are not absolute, it is still beneficial to be forwarned of their likelihood. Armed with such knowledge, we are able to anticipate, to make contingency plans, to prepare ourselves and possibly even deflect or prevent anything untoward from happening. On the plus side, this sort of predictive information can also help to encourage or confirm our decisions for the future.

Modern hand analysts have striven to repudiate the common fallacy that the lines in our hands never change, and that consequently we are stuck with what we are born with. Lines *can* and *do* change, for all sorts of reasons: according to our decisions, changes we make in our way of life, new influences that have an impact upon us or because of the state of our health.

If we had no powers of intervention and no control over our lives, we would certainly be puppets in the laps of the gods. This is not the case: we have free will, and we can make choices. We have the power to control and direct the course of our lives. Perhaps we don't have *absolute* control, but we can, to a large extent, shape our own destinies. Analyzing our hands provides the knowledge we need to make the best possible decisions about our future.

To appreciate that our own past, present and future experiences are reflected in our own hands is one thing; to accept that external influences or events occurring to others which touch upon our lives should also be marked in our hands is quite another! We could perhaps imagine that our hands are like photographic plates which receive and imprint our own ideas, actions and decisions, and that (whether consciously or unconsciously) we have a certain awareness of the implications of these upon our future lives.

But how much more difficult it is to explain, and then to accept, that sudden, unexpected events which are outside our sphere of influence should also be imprinted in our hands. How is it possible, for example, for an individual to develop a marking in her hand which reveals that in three years' time she will, out of the blue, be made redundant? Or for a partner to present a trauma line now which predicts his wife's sudden death? Or for a successful businessman to show the mark of his bankruptcy in ten years' time?

Perhaps, one way to explain this phenomenon is through Jung's concept of the collective unconscious: the notion that we are all in some way mentally interconnected through our ancestral experiences. Or perhaps the concept of the Zeitgeist – the idea that we can all pick up the prevailing trends, the thoughts and feelings of our times – might suit the explanation better.

There is no doubt that such phenomena *do* occur in the hand. By constantly monitoring our own markings we can prepare ourselves so that the unforeseen is no longer perceived as an unknown threat, but becomes instead an advanced warning which can be treated as a challenge and dealt with accordingly.

EMOTIONAL UPHEAVALS

Look for and apply the timing gauge to:

- Trauma lines originating from the Mounts of Mars or Venus, which cut through the Life line and possibly the Fate, Head and Heart lines too.
- Islands – on the Life line (for possible ill-health); on the Head line (for worries or anxieties); on the Fate line (for financial problems).
- Stars – on the Life line (accident, sudden injury or acute bouts of ill-health); on the Head line (shock, or injury to the head); on the Fate line (surprise or shock).
- An exceptionally long 'marriage line' that runs across the Mounts of Mercury and Apollo and then drops down to cut through the Heart line. This is a sign of bereavement.
- Horizontal dashes across the fingertips.

MOVES, JOURNEYS, RELOCATIONS OR CHANGES OF LIFESTYLE

Look for and apply the timing gauge to:

- Branches that drop out of the Life line and sweep towards the centre of the palm or further out towards Luna.
- A seemingly short Life line, which is in fact simply a short section attached by a very fine line to a longer section further out in the centre of the palm.
- Breaks in, or overlapping sections of, the Fate line.
- Branches that spring out of the Life line and shoot up towards the Mount of Saturn.

INFLUENCES, RELATIONSHIPS AND MARRIAGE

Look for and apply the timing gauge to:

- Lines rising from the Luna area sweeping in towards the Fate line. Those that don't meet or that cut right across the Fate line denote broken relationships. Those that merge into the Fate line denote marriage.
- Lines that run parallel to the main Fate line.
- Branches that sweep out from *inside* the Life line and then run along parallel to it.
- A sister or parallel line to the Life line.

FRUSTRATIONS, OBSTACLES OR OPPOSITION

Look for and apply the timing gauge to:

- Bars that cut across the Fate line (occupational); across the Head line (personal or psychological); across the Life line from the family ring (family or parental interference).

ACHIEVEMENTS AND SUCCESSES

Look for and apply the timing gauge to:

- Branches that rise up from the Head line.
- Branches that rise up from the Fate line.
- Branches that rise up from the Life line.
- The development of the Sun/Apollo line.
- Stars on the Mounts of Jupiter, Apollo or Mercury.

CHANGE OF JOB, CAREER OR OCCUPATION

Look for and apply the timing gauge to:

- Breaks in the Fate line – a clean break (redundancy); overlapped break (a change from choice); a wide space between the overlaps (move to a new career); many breaks (vacillations, many different jobs).
- A kink in the Fate line (promotion, side-step, and so on).

HEALTH

Look for and apply the timing gauge to:

- Any changes in the actual composition of the lines, e.g. chaining, islanding, fuzzing, fraying, sudden breaks.
- The development of many fine ancillary lines covering the palms.
- The development of either vertical or horizontal dashes on the fingertips.
- Any unusual discoloration, either severe reddening, yellowing or bluing, of the skin and/or nails.
- Distinct fading of the main lines.

- Stars forming on any of the main lines *except the Apollo line*.
- Distortion or deformity of the nails.
- Deep (sometimes red) indentations in the lines of Life, Head or Heart that have not been caused through injury.

PERSONAL FULFILMENT

Look for and apply the timing gauge to:

- The development of the Sun/Apollo line.
- An Apollo line ending in a trident.
- A star on the Apollo line.
- Stars on the Mounts of Jupiter, Apollo or Mercury.
- Rising branches sweeping upwards from any of the main lines.

LUCKY BREAKS, MONEY, ETC.

Look for and apply the timing gauge to:

- A peacock's eye fingerprint pattern on the tips of the ring or little fingers.
- Star on the Apollo line or on the Apollo mount.
- Star on a line from the percussion sweeping up towards the Apollo mount.
- A star on the Mercury mount.
- A line from the Life or Head lines up to the Jupiter mount with a star in it.
- A line from inside the Life line with a star in it shooting up to either the Apollo or Mercury mount.
- Three parallel lines on the Apollo mount starting above the Heart line.
- A Fate line that swings over and ends on the Jupiter mount (Figure 45).

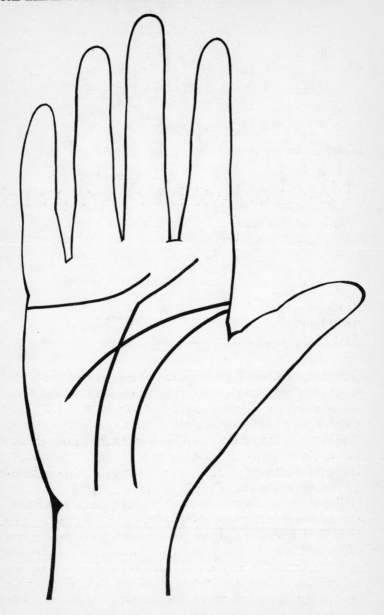

Figure 45. Fate Line Ending on the Mount of Jupiter

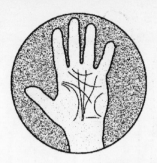

12 · EXAMPLE ANALYSES

CAREER OPTIONS

Rosie
Right-handed
Age: 14

Query: Rosie had reached the age where she had to take her school options, and so she had to decide which subjects she would drop and which she would take on to GCSE level. Essentially, should she follow a scientific pathway or favour the Arts? Whatever choices she made at this critical stage in her life would influence not only her A levels but, as a consequence, the type of career she would be able to follow for the rest of her life.

Clearly, then, what was required was to ascertain Rosie's potential and from there to establish which kinds of occupations would be most suited to her mentality and temperament. She would then be able to work out which subjects would be essential for her to take both at GCSE and at A Level. *Analytical procedure*: To gather information regarding suitability of occupation and career for an individual of this age, the areas to focus on are the hand shape, type and length of digits and phalanges, fingerprints and Head line.

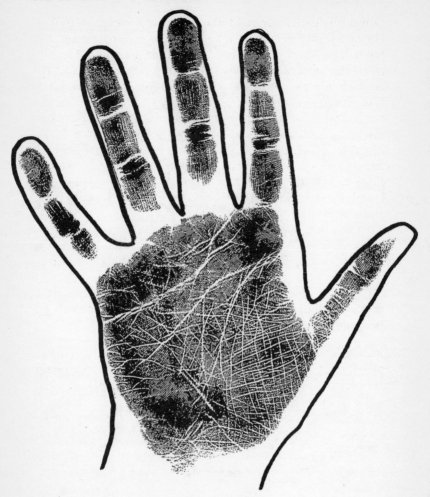

Print 14. Rosie

- Square palm long fingers = Air type = intellectual = communications
- Long second phalanx thumb = loves debate
- Good top phalanges of fingers = love of research
- Fingerprints majority = whorls = back-room girl, serious, deep thinker, confirms the love of research

- Composite pattern on right thumb = (can denote confusion) but excellent for making judgements, weighing matters in the balance = the law = barrister rather than solicitor
- Head line long and strongest line in hand = very intelligent, should go to university. Should consider postgraduate research towards PhD
- Head line = long. Note on left line begins straight as if drawn by a ruler until early thirties – subject says she loves physics – as Head line changes and sweeps down warned her that as she matures she will require scope for creative thinking. Whatever she does must have both structure and creativity together. With physics, then, perhaps could consider astronomy
- Air hand + creative bow = practical / intellectual / creative eye = engineering or architecture (shapely ring finger)
- Air hand = communications, gadgets = computers = information technology, neural networks
- Head line = half straight, half curved = softer sciences = medicine (but remember whorls) = medical research in preference to GP work

Common denominators: a need for structure with scope for creativity. A preference to work on her own. Ability to process data/information. Excellence at making judgements, solving problems. Intellectual. Academic.

Possible careers: law (barrister rather than solicitor); medical research; computer informatics; astronomy; engineering; architecture.

RELATIONSHIPS

Sally
Left-handed
Age: 35

Query: Sally has had several relationships of varying duration, each happy to begin with but then fizzling out for one reason or another. Sensing her biological clock ticking, she wondered if

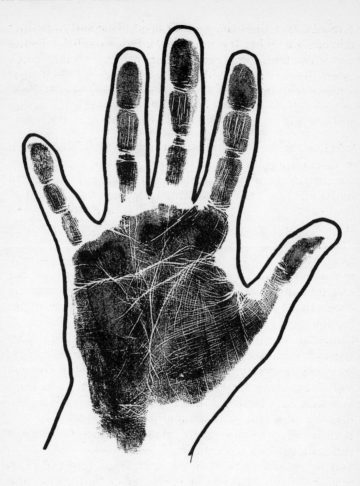

Print 15. Sally

she would ever find a long-term partner with whom she could share the rest of her life.

Analytical procedure: In a case such as this, the first step is to work out the individual's emotional pattern, how she interacts with and relates to others on a sexual level. The next step involves understanding her expectations: what sort of a relationship does she want or need, what sort of partner would be right for her. It is important here to establish whether she puts out the right signals, whether there is a mis-match between the person she believes herself to be and the picture she presents to the outside world. Finally, careful note must be taken of all relationship and/or influence markings together with the dates of their occurrence.

- Dominant Heart line straight but passive Heart line curved = discrepancy between a romantic, idealistic nature but the presentation of a self-sufficient, autonomous type of individual (e.g. Marilyn Monroe vs Margaret Thatcher!)
- Discrepant Heart lines = Sally needs a partner who is as strong as she is but who is also gentle and romantic underneath.
- Large Mount of Venus = Sally has a huge need to give love to another person, perhaps so much so that she loses her discriminative powers in a relationship and is consequently drawn to the wrong type of person: someone who consumes her love without giving the same amount back.
- Girdle of Venus = sensitivity but also negativity. This suggests negative expectations: e.g. *relationships* always *go wrong for me; I am unlucky; this relationship will not last.* Sally needs to put out more positive vibes and learn to believe in herself and in her ability to forge a strong and loving relationship with another person.
- Branch to Fate Line = strong evidence of potential partner. Branch joins Fate soon after mid-30s.
- Sun or Apollo lines = begin after Head line thus suggesting growth of sense of contentment, fulfilment, post mid-30s.
- Branch sweeping out from inside Life line = mark of a relationship circa 36/37.
- Sister line to Life line = at same time a sister line inside the Life line develops: one of the best signs of a strong influence/partnership.

Outcome: Given the analysis and a change of attitude, there is every indication that Sally will meet and form a strong relationship within the next twelve to eighteen months.

A HAPPY RETIREMENT

Bernard
Right-handed
Age: 66

Query: Following a long and distinguished career as a civil engineer, Bernard found his first year of retirement rather empty and unsatisfying. He was determined that these years should not be squandered, but that they should be as enriching and rewarding as his working years had been. He wanted to discover any inherent gifts and attributes which he could develop in order to make his retirement years special.

Analytical procedure: Natural gifts and talents in the hand are represented by special markings, by the skin patterns and by any unusual feature, whether of line delineation or physical construction that dramatically stands out. In this case Bernard had several strong formations which veritably *proclaimed* outstanding talents which he could happily employ to enrich his retirement years.

- Long top phalanges = love of research. The Saturn and Apollo nail phalanges are especially and unusually long – the former connected with the land and the latter with art and design.
- Formation of Apollo finger = eye for line and colour.
- Huge Mount of Luna = imagination.
- Bowed percussion = creativity.
- Head line = mathematical precision, obviously synonomous with his engineering work. However, evidence now of the Head line developing a creative fork.
- Majority of whorl fingerprints = loner, deep thinker.
- Low Luna skin loop = special rapport with Nature
- Low-placed Mount of Luna = closeness to the seasons, appreciation of Mother Nature, ability to pick up vibrations, sensitivity to the Earth.

Common denominators: art and design, the land, sensitivity to Nature.
Outcome: From this information two possible avenues emerged

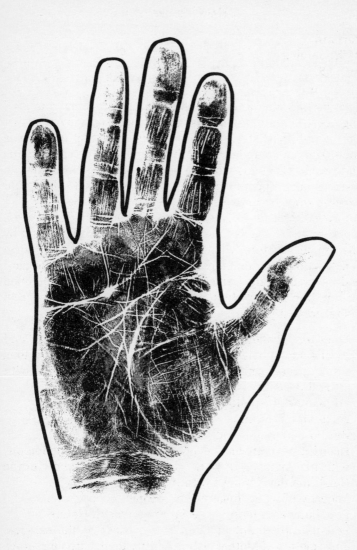

Print 16. Bernard

through which Bernard could express his talents. The first was landscape painting, and the second was landscape gardening.

As a result of the analysis Bernard has become a fine water-colourist, enjoying many days with easel and canvas painting spectacular scenes in the countryside. He is also researching for a book on gardens of a bygone age and plans to launch himself into designing historically thematic gardens.

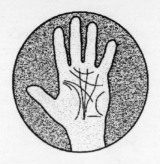

FURTHER READING

Altman, N., *Discover Palmistry*, Aquarian Press, 1991.

Altman, N & Fitzherbert, A., *Palmistry: Your Career in Your Hands*, Aquarian Press, 1988.

Benham, William G., *The Laws of Scientific Hand Reading*, Putnam, 1958.

Brandon-Jones, David, *Practical Palmistry*, Rider, 1981.

Fitzherbert, Andrew, *Hand Psychology*, Angus & Robertson, 1986.

Gettings, Fred, *The Book of the Hand*, Hamlyn, 1965.

Hutchinson, Beryl, *Your Life in Your Hands*, Sphere Books, 1967.

Jacquin, Noel, *The Hand of Man*, Faber & Faber, 1933.

Reid, Lori, *The Female Hand*, Aquarian Press, 1986.

— *The Complete Book of the Hand*, Pan, 1991.

— *Health in Your Hands*, Aquarian Press, 1993.

Warren-Davis, D., *The Hand Reveals*, Element, 1993.

INDEX